Devotional Companion
to the
International Lessons
2005–2006

Usable with All Popular Lesson Annuals

Jeffrey A. Rasche

ABINGDON PRESS / Nashville

DEVOTIONAL COMPANION TO THE INTERNATIONAL LESSONS 2005–2006

Copyright © 2005 by Abingdon Press

All rights reserved.
No part of this work may be reproduced or transmitted in any form or by any means, electronic or mechanical, including photocopying and recording, or by any information storage or retrieval system, except as may be expressly permitted by the 1976 Copyright Act or in writing from the publisher. Requests for permission should be addressed to Abingdon Press, P.O. Box 801, 201 Eighth Avenue South, Nashville, TN 37202-0801, or emailed to permissions@abingdonpress.com.

This book is printed on acid-free paper.

ISBN 0-687-04463-4
ISSN 1074-9918

Scripture taken from the Good News Translation in Today's English Version—Second Edition Copyright © 1992 by American Bible Society. Used by permission.

05 06 07 08 09 10 11 12 13 14 — 10 9 8 7 6 5 4 3 2 1

MANUFACTURED IN THE UNITED STATES OF AMERICA

Hymnals Referenced

B   Forbis, Wesley, ed. *The Baptist Hymnal.* Nashville: Convention Press, 1991.
C   *The Cokesbury Worship Hymnal.* Nashville: Abingdon Press, 1966.
E   Glover, Raymond, ed. *The Hymnal 1982.* New York: The Church Hymnal Corporation, 1985.
F   Bock, Fred, ed. *Hymns for the Family of God.* Nashville: Paragon Associates, Inc., 1976.
L   *Lutheran Book of Worship.* Minneapolis: Augsburg Publishing House, 1978.
P   McKim, LindaJo, ed. *The Presbyterian Hymnal.* Louisville: Westminster/John Knox Press, 1990.
UM Young, Carlton R., ed. *The United Methodist Hymnal.* Nashville: The United Methodist Publishing House, 1989.
W   Batastini, Robert J., ed. *Worship.* Chicago: GIA Publications, 1986.

READ IN YOUR BIBLE: *Psalm 16*   September 4, 2005
SUGGESTED PSALM: *Psalm 100*
SUGGESTED HYMNS:
  "Blessed Assurance" *(B, C, F, P, UM)*
  "Breathe on Me, Breath of God" *(B, E, F, L, P, UM, W)*

Encountering the Spirit

Hearing the Word

Psalm 16 rejoices in the presence of God. This is something that Christians should not take for granted; an important part of our Judeo/Christian faith is the belief that God is with us, and not some distant being (in some religions their god or highest power is not a "being" at all). Look at the verbs in Psalm 16; for example, this presence (of God) protects us, guides us, and fills us with joy. That is why Peter quoted this psalm (verses 8-11) in his speech to explain what happened on the Day of Pentecost; the Holy Spirit is the ongoing presence of God with us that protects, guides, and brings joy.

Living the Word

Recently we bought a new puppy; she is a Sheltie that looks like a five-inch-tall version of Lassie. In the books about the breed, we read that at about eight weeks old, puppies are especially vulnerable mentally. As they are weaned, they lose the close relationship they had with their mother, the giver and sustainer of their lives to that point. Therefore, they often feel afraid. They are small and not quite ready to deal with everything in the world. For example, the first time our puppy heard the phone ring in the kitchen, it surprised her so much she almost did a back flip trying to scramble away from it. They are losing their most important relationship in life, and in need of making new attachments to others (hopefully to their new owners). For the new owners, this is a time to build trust and begin a new and loving relationship with the puppy; to begin to know the puppy and to begin to guide the puppy in the expectations of its new family.

This "in-between stage" could describe the disciples after Jesus died. They too had lost the most important presence in their lives at that point, and felt vulnerable and alone in the world. They needed direction, guidance, empowerment, and new joy. But they waited, cowering like a frightened puppy behind closed and locked doors. Some of them apparently went back to fishing—their livelihood before they met Jesus. All of them had fled during the trial and crucifixion, and the closeness they had with the earthly Jesus was gone.

That is the emotional context of the coming of the Holy Spirit. To understand it helps explain the joy and euphoria they felt when the Spirit of God came upon them that first day. Instead of looking back with sadness at what they once had but now had lost, they could instead look with joy and enthusiasm and a sense of purpose at their new future with God.

There are many occasions in life when we may find ourselves or someone we love in an "in-between time." Grief is like that. So is divorce or retirement or the loss of a job. So is leaving home to go to college, or having a child leave home to go to college (something that many people are dealing with about this time of year). It is natural in the "in-between times" to look back at what we had, at all the security and comfort and joy that we must now leave behind. When we dare look ahead, it is unknown, and probably overwhelming, and probably frightening. We do not know yet what the "new normal" will be like.

This psalm, however, voices confidence in the fact that the God who has been there all along in our past will still go with us in the future. It is the feeling that is expressed in verse five, "You, LORD, are all I have, and you give me all I need; my future is in your hands."

At first, the puppy would not come out of the dog carrier we brought her home in. She sat in there, alone, and trembled. But we gently coaxed her out, and held her quietly for a long time, and have tried to come be with her even if she cries in the night. And now, when she hears our footsteps approaching, she still does her cute little cartwheels, but not from fear anymore. Now her leaping about is for pure joy; the kind of joy that gives us a glimpse of the joy that God has in store for us all one day, even on the other side of our "in-between" moments in life.

Let us pray:
Lord, help us to trust you when we experience moments of grief or fear, moments when we feel lost or alone. Today we especially pray for college students and their parents as they make their adjustments, and for all those who need your healing touch and your new joy. Amen.

READ IN YOUR BIBLE: *Romans 8:9-17*   September 11, 2005
SUGGESTED PSALM: *Psalm 133*
SUGGESTED HYMNS:
  "Holy, Holy, Holy" *(All)*
  "Blest Be the Tie That Binds" *(B, C, F, L, P, UM)*

Sharing Community

Hearing the Word

The book of Romans is perhaps the pinnacle of Paul's theological expression. It is put first in the order of Paul's books in the New Testament, but that is because his letters are arranged from the longest to the shortest. Most likely it was written late in his career, when his understanding was at a deep and rich point. He draws a sharp distinction between our human nature and the way of living by the Spirit. Living by the Spirit makes us God's children; living by our human nature leads to death. The lesson scripture today from Acts gives a glimpse of the radically different life the disciples led because of their union with God.

Living the Word

Today's lesson reading from Acts, if you really read it and understand it, should send a chill up your spine. After all, the disciples started off with the habit of selling everything they had and giving it all to the church to be redistributed to people as they had need. What if that practice had caught on?

One thing is sure; it would take a lot less time to count up the number of people who are church members. How many of your friends would still join the church if, in order to join, you had to have a giant yard sale and give up all your stuff? And imagine the interest this situation would generate at church council meetings, since the church leaders decided who needed money to buy a new car this month, and who could just get by fixing up their old one. It seems like there is enough haggling over money every month in church basements across the land already, even though our average personal stake in the matter is only 2 to 3 percent, if you can believe the folks who study church giving. What if we all were 100 percent invested in the church, and the church council determined what personal possessions we deserved. Why, it would probably lead to all-out war.

It's kind of fun to explore this idea, but it is a relief that communal possessions did not catch on for most of the church. Still, it does serve to make a point. The disciples believed that we Christians are entirely different people because of Christ, and they thought our lives should express that fact. They thought people in the world should look at us and see that we are different. Since we are no longer different from the rest of the world in our use of money, our devotional text (Romans 8:9-17) helps us see what really makes us different.

It is often difficult to distinguish, in terms of lifestyle, between a Christian and a non-Christian. Many Christians today choose not to talk about their faith verbally; they "let their actions speak." Unfortunately, we might be a little overconfident about how loudly our actions speak. If our lives are not too outwardly distinguishable from non-Christians who are also trying to be good people, then we just become silent sermonizers.

So maybe the idea of church members selling all their possessions would be a little more eye-catching. It would certainly help set us apart from the other "good people" in the world. But I don't think this devotional is going to be long enough to convince many people to sell all they have. So since we keep most of our possessions for ourselves (if you believe the researchers who say that on average mainline Christians give 2 to 3 percent to the church), we may want to find something else that sets us apart. It is not our moral life, nor our group economics.

No, we have not kept up with the early disciples in living a communal life that is shocking to the world. They might have been able to claim that their actions speak louder than words. As for us, the one thing that makes all the difference is not our good and upright life, as much as we would like to believe that; rather, it is the Spirit of God that forgives us, strengthens us, comforts us, guides us, saves us, and sends us out into the world to serve him.

Let us pray:

Lord, help us seek, and receive with joy, your Holy Spirit in our life today. May your Spirit work through us, and our churches, to do your will on earth as it is done in heaven. Through Christ our Lord, Amen.

READ IN YOUR BIBLE: *Luke 7:18-23* September 18, 2005
SUGGESTED PSALM: *Psalm 118:19-29*
SUGGESTED HYMNS:
  "Hope of the World" *(E, F, P, UM, W)*
  "Open My Eyes, That I May See" *(B, C, F, P, UM)*

The Gift of Healing

Hearing the Word

The most obvious connection between today's devotional and lesson scriptures is healing. In Acts 3:1-16, the disciples healed a lame man at the entrance to the temple; in Luke 7:18-23 Jesus tells John's disciples to answer John's question whether Jesus was in fact the Messiah with the facts, among other things, that people are being healed. Underlying the physical healings in each case, however, is a spiritual healing. Both incidents show how doubt or despair can change into faith and action. Jesus knew that John's question betrayed his doubts about Jesus. Likewise, in the aftermath of the healing, Peter confronted the doubts of his fellow Jews and invited them to believe in Jesus too.

Living the Word

One morning after a deep snow covered the ground, a father and his five-year-old son stepped outside. After one look at the large drifts of snow, the son said, "Dad, would you go first and take small steps so I can walk in your footprints?" Sometimes we all need another person to walk ahead of us.

Do you have someone like that in your life—someone you look up to like a mentor? In many ways, John the Baptist was that kind of person for Jesus. His role in Jesus' life was not limited to preaching in the wilderness shortly before Jesus' ministry began. The angels announced John's and Jesus' births, and John was identified as one who "prepared the way for the Lord" even before either of them had been born. John's path-finding work did not end when, as adults, he baptized Jesus. A careful reading of the Gospels shows that even after Jesus was baptized, he did not begin to preach until John had been imprisoned. When John's voice was silenced by prison, Jesus began to preach (it is interesting to note that Jesus' message is at that point almost identical to John's—see Matthew 4:12-17). Finally, after John was beheaded, note carefully the reaction of Jesus (see Matthew 14:1-13 and 16:21–17:13). Jesus grieved. John's death must have made him realize that he too would die a death like John's—an innocent and holy man put to death unjustly at the hands of his enemies. That is probably why Jesus started talking about his own death shortly after John's death, and why it was soon after John's beheading that Jesus went up the mountain at the transfiguration, where he changed course in his life's work and began to head for Jerusalem.

All this is to put John's question in its proper context. John was an important mentor to Jesus, even though he was still in prison at this point. John is the one who had first spoken of Jesus as the "Lamb of God" (see John 1:29-34). In the other Gospels John clearly realized that Jesus was God's Son too; that is why he thought Jesus should baptize him instead of the other way around. But this same John, one of the first people to believe in Jesus, and Jesus' God-given pathfinder, was now asking whether Jesus was the Messiah or whether someone else would come along who would be.

Even though it must have been disappointing to Jesus that John was asking this question, he told John's disciples to tell John about the fruits of Jesus' ministry. It was not meant to impress his mentor, but to help restore John's faith. The Bible is then silent about John's response. Was his faith in Jesus restored, or did he continue to doubt? I like to think that John's disciples helped John see God at work through Jesus. I hope that John went to his untimely and tragic death with a strong faith in Christ, and the knowledge that his path-finding work had been on target.

One of the insights we can gain from studying both of these stories (the lame man in Acts and the doubts of John the Baptist), is that *Jesus put the healing power of words and touch in the hands of others.* How often could you and I, with an outstretched hand in Jesus' name, help someone to his or her feet, or with our words help restore hope and faith in another person?

Let us pray:
   Lord, open my eyes today to see those with downcast eyes; open my heart today to feel the pain of those with heavy hearts. Open my hand that I may lift others to their feet. Open my mouth to share your love with them, that they may be strengthened and healed in your name. Amen.

READ IN YOUR BIBLE: *Ephesians 6:10-20* September 25, 2005
SUGGESTED PSALM: *Psalm 30*
SUGGESTED HYMNS:
  "Stand Up, Stand Up for Jesus" (B, C, E, F, L, UM)
  "Let All the World in Every Corner Sing" (B, C, E, P, UM, W)

Power to Be Bold

Hearing the Word

The theme that unites today's lesson scripture and today's devotional scripture is boldness to proclaim God's message in spite of opposition. In Ephesians, Paul is writing from prison, where his message has landed him. In spite of his bleak circumstances, he encourages his readers to "put on the armor of God," which is an analogy that has special meaning to those who feel they are under attack or in unfriendly territory. Paul ends this portion of his letter asking that his readers pray that Paul will continue to be bold in proclaiming the message of Christ. Likewise, Peter and John in Acts were facing opposition by the Sadducees and other Jewish authorities; knowing about Jesus' treatment at their hands, they were familiar with the threat, but they also sought boldness to prevent their fears from stopping them.

Living the Word

One of the general cultural characteristics of Midwesterners is that we often avoid direct conflict. Perhaps it is because farming people, who are tied to the land, have a vested interest in not antagonizing others in the community. But when we disagree with someone, it is easier to talk about it to someone besides the person with whom we disagree. Of course this is a generalization; there are certainly individuals who don't mind telling you to your face that you're wrong. And not having lived in other parts of the country, maybe this is a quirk of Midwesterners. But this desire to avoid conflict gets in the way of boldness.

Boldness requires that one person knowingly confront another with a thought or idea that might get a bad response. This is different than being obnoxious; to be obnoxious you have to add rudeness and insensitivity to boldness. Christians need the ability to distinguish between that which is unhelpful and unwelcome, and that which is unwelcome but still helpful.

Paul's message was certainly "unwelcome" to many people. But since it was given to them with their best interest at heart, it was bold.

Today, even the word "evangelism" has become unwelcome to many people. Some television evangelists, with their transparent attempts to get money and their eccentric, even criminal behavior, have made the Christian message "unwelcome" to many unchurched people. Unfortunately, for many in the TV channel-surfing public, "evangelism" has become associated with pushiness, insincerity, rudeness, wild hair, bad makeup, and money-grubbing for such "people-helping" purposes as purchasing a new satellite for their show.

Now, is there any possibility that anybody in your community feels this same way about your church? For example, if the only letter they ever get from your church is the annual "Please give more money this year" letter, and they never have a hint that people in the church want to be of service to them?

It is difficult to approach people who may find the Christian message unwelcome, who may associate it with money-grubbing and self-serving institutions. You have to be bold to do it—you have to go into territory where you know you are unwelcome, but where the message you have is still necessary and helpful.

Thus, the most basic question is this: Do you think people need to hear the message of Christ for their own good, or not? If not, then it is better to leave them to their channel surfing. But if you believe they do need Christ and the fellowship of the church, then you might have to be bold enough to overcome whatever barriers they have put up, and seek to serve them.

The church has one thing that no TV show can ever have. In the church, we can offer a truly personal approach even to those who do not welcome the church.

Let us pray:
Lord, help us be bold enough to speak out for you, even when we know that someone may hear who does not share our faith. May our love and our service give us the opportunity to share your message in places where it would not otherwise be heard. In Christ we pray, Amen.

READ IN YOUR BIBLE: *Isaiah 6:1-8* October 2, 2005
SUGGESTED PSALM: *Psalm 131*
SUGGESTED HYMNS:
  "Be Thou My Vision" *(B, E, F, P, UM)*
  "O God, Our Help in Ages Past" *(All)*

Faithful Servant

Hearing the Word

Isaiah had quite a vision, didn't he? He saw the Lord seated in glory in his heavenly court. Note that he was amazed that he could see God and still live; it was thought that for any mortal to see God would result in instant death. That is why even the heavenly beings used one pair of their wings to cover their faces.

This passage is sometimes known as "the call of Isaiah." You might want to compare it to the call stories of the two other major prophets, Jeremiah (Jeremiah 1:4-10) and Ezekiel (Ezekiel 1:28*b*–3:15). Isaiah's call is given in a general way, like asking a crowd who will volunteer, but Isaiah offers his services. Likewise, just before today's lesson scripture begins, Stephen has been chosen to help the apostles. He goes on to be the first Christian martyr, and his death has many similarities to that of Jesus'.

Living the Word

One of the fun daily rituals in a small town is the noon whistle. No matter what the family dog is doing at that moment, when the great whistle blows, the ears snap to attention. She looks intently in the general direction of the whistle, listening carefully to its blaring, rising wail. Finally, in response to the initial call from the invisible great dog with the powerful voice, dogs all over town turn their faces skyward and answer with howls of their own. For a few moments, as the great voice dims to a low hum, canines from all over town take up the song.

Maybe they think it is the forlorn call for help from a great dog that is lost. So they howl, in dog solidarity, to say, "Hey, the rest of the gang is over here!" Maybe they think of it much like we think

Devotional Companion to the International Lessons

of choir practice. The leader shows us how to sing, and then the choir sings. Or perhaps it is some form of entertainment.

The siren has an important message for humans too. In many small towns, if it goes off anytime besides noon or six o'clock, it either means that there is a tornado warning or that the volunteer fire department is being called into service.

In the old days, before sirens, God relied on visions to call people into service. Now that we live in an electronic age, we have a lot of ways to hear God's call. We have telephones, cell phones, beepers, radio, television, and even the Internet. Isaiah had none of these modern conveniences. Still, he had a vision in which he felt God's calling, and he answered that call. In agreeing to be God's representative, he became a truly great and longtime prophet; his writing includes the treasured vision of the suffering servant, the idea of the peaceable kingdom, and great words of comfort and hope for his suffering people after the exile. His inspiring response to God's call, "Here am I, Lord, send me," has inspired a popular hymn and become a motto for mission work.

It is best, though, when those words become ours. "Here I am, Lord, send me." We might say that we haven't really heard God's call like Isaiah did; we have not had any visions of thrones or heavenly beings or booming voices. We may wonder what to do, or who needs our love and service in the world today. But in an age when we see world events in our living room as they unfold, God's call should not be too difficult to hear. When we consider how the whole continent of Africa is threatened by AIDS and hunger and poverty, when we realize that the majority of the homeless in America are children, when we learn to recognize the poor or lonely or grieving in our community, we have begun to hear the call of God.

And once we hear the call, it is up to us, wherever we may be and whatever we may be doing, to respond. After all, every day at noon and six, even the dogs in town perk up their ears, listen carefully, and answer the call.

Let us pray:
Lord, we know that you continue to speak to people, creating opportunities for us to work with you side by side. May we hear your call, and instead of thinking of someone else to do the job, say in our heart, "Here I am, Lord, send me." Amen.

READ IN YOUR BIBLE: *Acts 19:1-10* October 9, 2005
SUGGESTED PSALM: *Psalm 27*
SUGGESTED HYMNS:
  "In Christ There Is No East or West" *(All)*
  "My Hope Is Built on Nothing Less" *(B, C, F, L, P, UM)*

Christians Without Borders

Hearing the Word

This passage is rich with important subjects to understand. First, it is a great example of how Paul went about his work in a new city. Second, it details some of the difficulties he faced (trying to convince stubborn or even hostile unbelievers, cleaning up after misinformed teachers). Third, because Paul needed to correct the baptism that the believers in Ephesus had received from Apollos, it provides an excellent opportunity to come to a deeper understanding of baptism, speaking in tongues, and receiving the Holy Spirit. Finally, remembering that we have Paul's letter to the Ephesians, having this record of the beginnings of Paul's relationship with that church helps place that book of the Bible in context.

Living the Word

I heard a woman comment about her husband, "He doesn't always agree with me, but I tell him that's all right. After all, America's a free country, so he has the freedom to be wrong."

Probably marriage is the number one context for disagreement; but the church would be a close runner-up. Paul and Apollos were not the first ones to disagree on what baptism means, and certainly they were not the last. Even Jesus and John the Baptist seemed to have different understandings about baptism, which is why John the Baptist nearly refused to baptize Jesus (he thought of baptism more like Apollos apparently did, which was a rite for the washing away of sins, while to Jesus, it was apparently more of a sign of relationship with God—thus the voice from heaven saying that Jesus was God's son).

The reason we have so many different denominations is because at least historically, Christians disagreed with one another to the extent that they concluded that they needed whole separate churches in order to carry on their work. Those churches are always out there, spreading their ideas and conducting the sacraments according to their beliefs. For example, it is not uncommon for a youth who was baptized as an infant to go to a Bible camp or revival at a friend's church, and come home with the idea that their baptism as an infant didn't really count and they should be re-baptized, disputed by many denominations.

We live in a milieu of ideas—religious, political, and otherwise. Even when Paul went to the church at Ephesus, he was not the first one to share his ideas. He had to compete with the ideas that Apollos had taught earlier. In fact, you do not have to read Paul's letters too long to come across his warnings about "false teachers." When we in the church reach out to others, especially to the unchurched, we have to accept the reality that we are not speaking into a vacuum. There is already a preexisting set of ideas and assumptions to deal with.

It is a challenge to listen to the ideas of others with respect. It can be difficult to decide what ideas we can live with and what ones we should seek to correct in someone else. But that is a problem. Most of the people we think are misled are equally sure we are wrong, and are committed to correcting us.

You wonder what God thinks about it all. God knows our thoughts: those who are pro-choice and pro-life, those who are for infant baptism and those who are for believer's baptism, those who are Cub fans and those who are Cardinal fans, those who are fiercely local to their mainline Protestant church and those who have been lifelong Catholics and those nondenominational folks who disagree with the disagreements between denominations. But God has given us freedom of thought. That includes the freedom to be wrong. So I hope I'm right about everything. But in case I'm not entirely right about that, I believe in a God who loves us for more than the correctness of our ideas. God loves us for who we are, the diverse people that God has made.

Let us pray:
Lord, help me really listen to someone today who has a radically different point of view than I do, and practice loving them as a person in spite of our differences. Amen.

READ IN YOUR BIBLE: *Acts 11:19-26*   October 16, 2005
SUGGESTED PSALM: *Psalm 147*
SUGGESTED HYMNS:
  "There Is a Balm in Gilead" *(B, E, F, P, UM, W)*
  "Come, Thou Fount of Every Blessing" *(B, C, E, F, L, P, UM)*

Interpreting the Word

Hearing the Word

One of the important contributions of the book of Acts is to show us how the Christian faith grew beyond a group of twelve disciples firmly entrenched in the heart of Jewish country to reach the rest of the world. The lesson and devotional texts show the gospel going beyond the bounds of the Jewish community, and spreading to Gentiles (non-Jews). This reveals one of the underlying theological beliefs of Luke (who wrote Acts), which is that Jesus' life and death and resurrection was for all people, and not just the Jewish people (note how Luke's genealogy in Luke 3:23-38 goes back to Adam, the ancestor all humans have in common; while Matthew's genealogy in Matthew 1:1-17 begins with Abraham, the father of the Jews).

Living the Word

It was a startling, and thought-provoking video—one of those moments that change the way you see the world. At a denominational conference, delegates were treated to a series of videos interpreting some of the ministries of the conference that all churches support with their "conference claims" dollars.

The last of the series appeared to be plagued by technical difficulties. The video showed a worship service in progress, but the sound was not working. You could see a choir singing and swaying, the band playing their instruments, a drummer pounding out a rhythm, the congregation clapping, and a preacher proclaiming a message. After a minute or two of this, you could see people at the conference look impatiently back in the direction of the sound and video technicians. Their looks were saying, "Fix the sound. Can't you see it's not working?" The crowd began to murmur.

Suddenly, the video cut to one of our ministers who works with the deaf and hearing-impaired. He himself is completely deaf. In sign language, which was subtitled for those of us who do not understand ASL (American Sign Language), he told the delegates that this is the way deaf people experience our worship services. It is frustrating to see everyone laugh at a joke the preacher tells, but not have any idea why people are laughing. He told us that for many deaf people, singing has little or no meaning because they have never heard music, and so it is boring to sit through a song that you cannot hear or appreciate. These reasons, plus the social barriers that exist between the hearing and nonhearing worlds, keep the deaf isolated in our own midst. They feel they cannot participate in the local church, and even in those rare cases when it is signed for them by a church-paid interpreter, so many people in the congregation cannot communicate with them that it is difficult to feel a part of the life of the congregation. He explained that because of their isolation, many deaf people have never heard the basic Bible stories that the rest of us received in childhood through Sunday school, children's books, vacation Bible school, and so on.

As he "talked" to us with ASL, that crowd fell completely silent. For a moment, a wall was torn down, and we in the hearing majority were given a precious lesson about the life of the deaf and hearing-impaired minority in our own communities.

I wonder; would the early church leaders like Barnabas and Peter and the apostle Paul have assumed that since they never saw deaf people in church that they were just not interested in receiving the gospel? I don't think so. They were the kind of Christians we should all be; not content merely to reach out to their own people. They looked for all the ways possible to make their community accessible and welcoming and inclusive of everyone, Jewish or Gentile. Perhaps today that means more of us need to know ASL, and about other handicapping conditions, and open the church doors in new ways.

Let us pray:
Lord, forgive us for limiting the church community, for being content when our worship and programs fail to include everyone. Forgive us for thinking that it is not "cost-effective" to reach out to a minority of people in our area with the gospel of Jesus Christ. Heal us of our blindness and deafness, and restore a full and complete community to your church in every place. Amen.

READ IN YOUR BIBLE: *Acts 13:44-49* October 23, 2005
SUGGESTED PSALM: *Psalm 27*
SUGGESTED HYMNS:
 "Dear Lord and Father of Mankind" (B, C, E, F, L, P, UM)
 "Sing Praise to God Who Reigns Above" (B, E, F, P, UM, W)

Breaking the Gospel Barriers

Hearing the Word

Today's devotional and lesson texts indicate that the early church's big issue was whether or not to include the Gentiles (non-Jews). Paul and Barnabas were early proponents of taking the Christian faith to the Gentiles, and at first Peter (Jesus' handpicked leader from his disciples) thought it was a message for the Jewish people only. Paul and Barnabas quoted Isaiah's preaching (see 42:6 and 49:6) that Israel should be a light to the nations. This self-understanding of Israel's purpose was one view; surely either there were those who understood Israel's mission differently, didn't think it should be in mission beyond itself, or who believed they should be a light to the nations but did not practice that belief.

Living the Word

A single frame cartoon without a cpation pictures a wide-eyed caretaker charging up the steps of a lighthouse. A huge ocean-going ship is quite close, bearing down on him, about to knock the lighthouse down. In his arms, he is carrying a box containing a new bulb, and frantically hoping to change it before it is too late.

That image may capture an indictment of the church, both in Paul's day and today. A lighthouse with a burned out light. We have the buildings, but there are ways we have let the light go out. As children in vacation Bible school, we sing "This little light of mine, I'm gonna let it shine." We say we won't hide it, we won't put it under a bushel, and we won't let Satan blow it out. But then we grow up, and we have a different perspective. Our culture, our race, our economic strata, our handicapping conditions, and other factors influence it.

Should we spend $25,000 to add a chairlift to the building when nobody in a wheelchair comes to church right now? ("If they do come, we can carry them up the steps a lot cheaper than putting that thing in.") Of course, probably the reason they don't come is because being carried up the steps by a bunch of guys while you sit in your wheelchair is totally demeaning. And regarding race, it continues to be an affront to the kingdom of God that the most segregated hour in America is Sunday morning worship. This is true not just for racial differences, but also for economic class. There are exceptions of course, but if an alien came to study the church in the United States, without having a clue about our mission and purpose, and about who was included in our fellowship, then what would they conclude after studying your church building, your habits, your congregational makeup, your church budget, and your agenda at board meetings?

At most of the churches I have served or known about, the finance report is typically first on the agenda. The missions and evangelism reports came later in the meeting. Everyone around the table, no matter what committee they represented, wrote down the current numbers of the finance report. We all want to know how much money we have, but hardly any notes are taken about the evangelism or mission reports. We get in animated conversations about what color to paint the men's room (even the woman had an opinion) or what to do when we are falling a little behind in the budget (as we do every year in the summer, only to catch up every fall). But during the missions and evangelism reports, which talk about how many people we are trying to reach for Christ or serve in Christ, not a note is taken.

We still have the same struggle in the church today that Paul and Barnabas had then. We are tempted to be provincial, to care about our own building, our own community, and our own people, however we define that group. But we better remember that the purpose of a lighthouse is to "let this little light shine." The purpose of the church is no different.

Let us pray:
Lord, take our gaze off the church building and budget once in a while, so that we may see the people of our community and world, their need of you, and their need for love and service, in order that, following you, we may become a light to the world, and lead many people to you. In Christ, Amen.

READ IN YOUR BIBLE: *Psalm 46* **October 30, 2005**
SUGGESTED PSALM: *Psalm 47*
SUGGESTED HYMNS:
  "Guide Me, O Thou Great Jehovah" (B, C, E, F, P, UM)
  "Praise to the Lord, the Almighty" (B, E, F, L, P, UM, W)

Never Alone

Hearing the Word

Psalm 46, like a hymn, can be divided into three verses with a refrain. The first verse (vv. 1-3) is about God's presence in spite of destruction and disaster; the images could be compared with that of the flood story in Genesis. The second verse (vv. 4-6) expresses confidence in the temple and the ongoing city of God, which could be understood to be Jerusalem. The third verse (vv. 8-10) is a vision of the future, when conflicts cease and all people worship Israel's one God. The refrain (vv. 7 and 11) is at the end of the second and third verses.

Living the Word

A boy, sitting quietly in church next to his parents, suddenly let out a shrill, two-finger-in-the-mouth whistle. It stopped the worship service cold. Everyone, including the preacher, stared at the boy and waited for an apology or explanation. The boy said simply but with a triumphant grin, "It's a miracle! For weeks I've been praying for God to teach me to whistle, and God did just then."

One of the most famous verses in the Bible comes from verse 10 of this psalm. The New Revised Standard Version translation reads, " 'Be still, and know that I am God.' " The Good News Translation, perhaps taking its cue from the context of verses 8-9, reads, " 'Stop fighting,' he says, 'and know that I am God.' " There are other ways to translate this verse, but they all convey the thought that no matter what happens, we need to keep the perspective that God is with us and because of that, trouble and turmoil can be replaced by peace and stillness.

Devotional Companion to the International Lessons

Sometimes when I was worried about something, my grandmother would say, "Be still now. Don't worry about that." Then when we siblings were fighting with each other, she would say, "Be still now. Quit fighting." At the time, I got the idea that she was hoping for grandchildren who didn't move around much, that we had to be still physically. Over the years, I have come to realize that her saying was related to Psalm 46. It is not talking about physical activity, but a quieting of the spirit.

Even as adults, we fuss and fight and worry about so many things. We accumulate them in our memories as though they would make a great book of life. Eventually those things will not matter. In the end, what matters most is the reality we currently experience—the simple truth that God is with us. To know this, and deeply believe it, places all of life in a different context. It means that we are not alone, that we don't have to rely on only ourselves, and that God cares enough to bring us through every challenge we face, no matter how great it may be.

War, hurricanes, earthquakes, bad news, grief, job loss, fear, divorce, and even death—any of these things can turn our life upside down and might even destroy our life as we know it. All of these forces are part of life, and all of them are frightening to most of us. But none of these forces are greater than God of all creation. The simple affirmation of Psalm 46 is that God is with us. God is not in the storm and the destruction and the fighting, but God is there for the healing, the quieting down, the recovery, and the resurrection.

You or someone you love may be facing difficult news today. You might not have slept a wink all night, and for good reason. But no matter how disturbed and upsetting your circumstances may be, try to remember that all storms end, that peace eventually overtakes all wars, that no problems last forever, and that even death itself is swallowed up in the final victory of resurrection. My grandma knew that and taught it to me. God is with us. Try to be still, and know that God is with us.

Let us pray:
Lord, thank you for being there through it all. Thank you that you love us and care for us enough to solve every problem we face, and that one day all such strife and worry will give way to perfect, stress-free, eternal life in your loving presence. Amen.

READ IN YOUR BIBLE: *Acts 9:23-31*   November 6, 2005
SUGGESTED PSALM: *Psalm 137*
SUGGESTED HYMNS:
 "In Christ There Is No East or West" *(All)*
 "Let Us Break Bread Together" *(B, E, F, L, P, UM, W)*

Encountering Truth

Hearing the Word

It is hard to believe the contrast between today's lesson scripture and today's devotion scripture, especially because both are located in the same chapter of Acts. In one, Paul is the persecutor; in the other, he is persecuted. In one, he is zealously against Christians; in the other, he is on his way to becoming a great Christian leader. In the lesson text, Paul was working to weaken and shrink the church, but as our devotional scripture concludes, the church is being strengthened and is growing in numbers. What is the difference? It is the intervention of God, and the conversion of Saul (later Paul) from a great Christian persecutor into a great Christian leader.

Living the Word

As this is being written, the news is breaking on television of the second American hostage in the recent past that was abducted in Saudi Arabia by Islamic extremists and then beheaded. Photos and videotape of the beheadings were posted on an extremist Islamic Web site for the world to see; the images were so gruesome that even the news networks decided not to replay them. In the aftermath, some of our political leaders called our enemies "savages," and "terrorists." They vowed to track down the killers and punish them. We will certainly feel justified in punishing those brutal thugs for beheading an American civilian.

In reaction to this brutal and televised murder, some people here in America have leaped to the conclusion that "they are animals—they are not like us." We have bought the idea that "they" are less than human or in some way lower or different than we are. In spite of the horrendous nature of their behavior, though, it is important for Christians, and part of "loving our enemies," to not give in to the (understandable) urge to view our enemies as sub-human beings. We do not have to feel love, but we owe it to God, who made them like God made us, to at least seek to find such Christian concepts as understanding and peace and even forgiveness and reconciliation.

Paul's life in this chapter is a case in point. At the beginning of the chapter, he was an adamant Christian persecutor. By the end of the chapter, he had changed sides completely. Yet it is his view of the people on the other side that is of special interest. When he was against Christians, he was ready to kill them. We might say his goal was to rid them from society. He clearly hated Christians and approved of Stephen's stoning (a method of killing that is just as barbaric as beheading).

Paul's "pre-Christian" view of his enemy is the normal human point of view. They are bad. They are different from "normal" people like us. Therefore we should kill them and not feel bad about it. Perhaps the point could be summarized by a war veteran who, when asked by a journalist whether he ever felt bad for killing so many of his enemy, looked at her incredulously and replied something to the effect of, "No. The only thing I ever felt bad about is that I did not manage to kill a hundred times as many."

So, how did Paul seem to feel about his "enemy" when he switched sides? He understood them well, because he had once been one of them. He went to them, spoke to them, argued his point of view to them, but he never advocated that they be killed. Even when his enemies whipped him, imprisoned him, chased him out of town, insulted him, and even tried to kill him, he continued to treat them with respect and to remember that they were still human beings that God created. He knew that they needed to hear the gospel, but one thing that changed when he became Christian was more than the side he fought for; it changed the way he understood and treated his enemies. It is a good lesson for us to remember, particularly in times of war and hatred and yes, even obscenely brutal beheadings.

Let us pray:
Lord, when the phrase "love your enemies" seems impossible to do, help us at least find a way to resist the corrosion of blinding generalized anger and hatred. We pray today for the seemingly distant dreams of peace and reconciliation. Amen.

READ IN YOUR BIBLE: *Acts 16:25-34* November 13, 2005
SUGGESTED PSALM: *Psalm 107:1-22*
SUGGESTED HYMNS:
  "Come Down, O Love Divine" *(E, L, P, UM, W)*
  "Love Divine, All Loves Excelling" *(All)*

Offering of Oneself

Hearing the Word

Both the lesson scripture (the conversion of Lydia) and the devotion scripture (the conversion of the jailor) include the subsequent baptism of whole households. This is one of the scriptural arguments given by those who practice infant baptism, since most other recorded baptisms (including Jesus') were done for adults. However, the reason these passages were linked today is because following their respective conversions, Lydia and the jailor offered their home to Paul and his traveling companions. Note that the lesson scripture contains one of Acts "we" passages. Verses 16:6-9 tell the story using the third-person "they." Suddenly in verse 10 and following, the story is told from the first-person "we." This shift has been a point of discussion for scholars. Did Luke incorporate someone else's first-person account, or is there some other reason for the shift of view? There are other places in Acts where this occurs; look for them and see what you conclude.

Living the Word

On their twenty-fifth wedding anniversary reception, a woman suddenly broke into sobs. Her friend took her aside and asked her why she was crying. She replied, "I have a miserable marriage. My husband runs around on me, he has never once said he loved me or brought me flowers, he treats me like dirt, and the worst part is that I knew all this by the time we got to our fifth wedding anniversary."

"But why are you crying now?" the friend persisted.

"Because, on our fifth wedding anniversary, I was planning to poison him. But I asked our friend, the one who is a lawyer, how long someone would get in prison for poisoning her husband, and she said, 'Oh, about twenty years.'"

She broke down in fresh sobs, and finally wailed through her tears, "That means if only I had carried out my plan, I'd be a free woman today."

Marriage is meant to be a blessing, but sadly, in some cases it can be like a prison. There are other situations in life that feel like that. For example, some jobs seem like dead-end streets without escape, and some people who suffer from various diseases or conditions are like prisoners in their own bodies. Then, of course, some people, like Paul and Silas in our scripture lesson today, really are prisoners.

If you read the story carefully, you will see that Paul and Silas were not the only prisoners. The jailor was also a prisoner, but his prison was different. When the prison doors were opened, the jailor was in mortal fear for his life, and even considered suicide. It is not a stretch to see that he was in an oppressive job situation. He was also a spiritual prisoner. He must have heard Paul and Silas talking and singing earlier, and been interested enough to listen carefully and give their ideas some thought, because this is a case when, before the sermon instead of after it, he asked, "What must I do to be saved?" It was as though he blurted out the question in desperation. He was not only in need of a new and better job, but a new and better spiritual life.

That is why the jailor's story is one we can all identify with, for like him, it is God who has set us free. Our sins, and sometimes the circumstances of our lives, could be understood as a prison. They are imposed unwillingly on us, and we do not have the power on our own to escape. Like the earthquake that God used to free Paul and Silas, God will find a way to free us from our shackles. Our sins were leading us not only to prison, but to the death penalty. But God sent Jesus to set the prisoners free.

With God, all shackles, including sin and death itself, will one day fall away, and in Christ, we will truly be free.

Let us pray:

Lord, be with those who are in prison today, and those whose prisons in life have made them lose hope. Thank you for the freedom we have through Jesus Christ to receive and live, no matter what our earthly circumstances, your gift of new life. Amen.

READ IN YOUR BIBLE: *Luke 10:1-11* November 20, 2005
SUGGESTED PSALM: *Psalm 27*
SUGGESTED HYMNS:
 "Take Up Thy Cross" *(B, E, L, P, UM, W)*
 "O Master, Let Me Walk with Thee" *(B, C, E, F, L, P, UM)*

Working Together in Ministry

Hearing the Word

In his instructions to the seventy-two men Jesus sent out two by two, he told them to find people who would work with them and support them in their ministry. As for those who would not support the disciples, Jesus had harsh words. He told them to shake the dust off their feet (see Paul's action of shaking the dust off his clothes in protest of the way he had been treated in Acts 18:6 and the surrounding context of today's lesson scripture). The sending out of the seventy-two is unique to Luke's Gospel, but remember that Luke also wrote Acts; he is particularly interested in showing how Jesus, and later Paul and the disciples, were intent on spreading the faith. The parallel between today's devotional and lesson texts is the way that missionaries worked together with the people in the community where they were serving.

Living the Word

A pastor got sick and wound up in a hospital. His condition was not serious, and he was expected to make a full recovery. During his third day in the hospital, a representative of his church board came to visit. "Here, pastor," he said, "I brought you a get-well card from the church board. At the meeting last night we voted on whether to send it, and the motion passed thirteen to twelve."

It kind of gives you a warm, fuzzy feeling inside, doesn't it? Of course, this story was just a joke, but there are plenty of poor relationships between pastors and churches that are no joke. There is an ongoing epidemic of pastoral moves. It is rare to see someone who has served the same community for ten years or more. Actually, staying longer than five years in one place is pretty unusual.

This is not a picture of healthy long-term relationships. Perhaps some pastors deliberately plan to spend just two or three years at each place, but more often this rapid movement is the sign of disappointment, anger, and general failure on the part of both churches and pastors to construct healthy, long-lasting relationships.

It is not usually productive to assign blame—that gives one side an excuse not to change. What is productive is for pastor and people to pay attention to their relationship, and practice love, forgiveness, kindness, and hospitality with each other.

When Jesus sought to prepare his disciples to go out, he let them know that serving a community can either be a blessing or an experience where, well, you want to shake the dust off your feet. One pastor I know described his second church appointment as "the armpit of America," and said, "I couldn't get out of there fast enough." When he left, at the end of his first year, he had everything packed in his car, waiting just outside the church door. He gave the final benediction, walked out the back door, got in his car, and never returned to that town. What does it mean to "shake the dust off"?

One aspect of it for Jesus was a visible warning to the people of the town that they needed to change. It was a prophetic act meant as a last-ditch effort, not to condemn them, but by warning them, to save them. It was an act of love even for those who acted like wolves around a sheep. But it was also therapeutic for his messengers to leave a rejection behind. By moving on, they had a chance to heal from the pain and find a more effective place to work.

In all walks of life, there are times to "shake the dust off." Painful experiences such as job loss or divorce or being victimized by crime are examples of occasions when we need to deal with, and then leave the experience behind, so we can move on. Many times we cannot avoid these experiences of pain and rejection. But when we must, Jesus' advice to "shake the dust off" and move on is sometimes the best we can do.

Let us pray:

Lord, be with our pastor, and with pastors everywhere. Help us support our pastor's good qualities and help her or him, with love and kindness, in areas that need improvement. Help pastors realize the sacred task they have been given, and feel grateful for the opportunity to serve your people. Amen.

READ IN YOUR BIBLE: *Acts 20:31-35*   November 27, 2005
SUGGESTED PSALM: *Psalm 23*
SUGGESTED HYMNS:
  "Blest Be the Tie That Binds" *(B, C, F, L, P, UM)*
  "There Is a Balm in Gilead" *(B, E, F, P, UM, W)*

Saying Good-bye

Hearing the Word

The lesson and devotional scriptures today come from Paul's farewell speech as he left Ephesus (the church to which he wrote the book of Ephesians). He has been there for three years (a long time for Paul, whose travels are extensive and incredible for a person in his day). His speech includes warnings against "wolves," which Jesus also used to describe the disciples' adversaries in last week's devotional scripture. Probably this meant either persecutors from outside the church or false teachers within the church. In his speech, Paul also mentions a famous saying of Jesus "There is more happiness in giving than in receiving" (20:35). It is not recorded in any of the Gospels, however it was a common saying in Jesus' day, and he could well have said it. Remember that Paul never personally met Jesus, so it is unusual for him to directly quote Christ like the Gospel writers did.

Living the Word

An older woman who died recently had a little quirk. She would never say "good-bye" on the phone. Everyone who knew her understood this, so they would end conversations by saying "See you later." I don't know if she just was uncomfortable with the word "good-bye" or whether to her "good-bye" was a theologically inappropriate concept.

When she died, everyone who knew and loved her had to say "good-bye" to her in some way. Some chose flowers, some came to visitation, and some attended the funeral. The preacher ended the funeral sermon by commenting on how she would say "See you later" instead of "Good-bye." He pointed out that with God there is no such thing as good-bye, for with God all endings are actually new beginnings. He ended the sermon with the words "see you later." This theological understanding should undergird all of our farewells. They are all temporary.

Whether our good-bye is because of a neighbor moving away or retirement or death, there are some good components of saying farewell that Paul models in his speech to the leaders of the church at Ephesus. Even the word "farewell" is a short way of saying "Fare thee well." It reveals the first important task of saying good-bye, and that is giving the other person your blessing.

A second aspect of Paul's farewell speech was to summarize the important things he wanted them to remember about the relationship he had with them. This can be as simple as ending a routine phone call with a summary statement like, "Well, I just wanted to wish you a happy birthday on your special day." It can be more difficult, like writing a poem about a person who died. But as a relationship or a part of one concludes, it is good to come to terms with what it has meant to you.

A third aspect of Paul's farewell was obviously showing a lot of emotion. Sometimes we try to stuff it in. However, God gave us our emotions. They have healing power. The refusal to grieve, for example, has been linked to higher rates of mental illness. So if something that matters to you is ending, such as a job you have loved for forty years or your child is moving out to go to college, then tears are fine. There are many ways to show emotion, but remember that even Jesus wept when his friend Lazarus died.

Learning to deal with separation is something we work on from the time we are babies. We can't avoid it in life. A lot of life is learning to say "hello" and "good-bye." Keep in mind what that preacher said at the end of the sermon for the woman who never would say "good-bye." Our good-byes are merely the ending of a middle chapter in life's book. The final chapter, written by God, is one in which all the people get together again, all the loves of our life will continue, and the hopeful words "see you later" are fulfilled.

Let us pray:
Lord, we pray for those who grieve today, whether because of job loss, moving, or death. Help us all appreciate the people in our life while they are with us, and learn to say "farewell" with love and grace when we must, hoping all the while that in you, we will one day meet again. Amen.

READ IN YOUR BIBLE: *Isaiah 41:8-13*   December 4, 2005
SUGGESTED PSALM: *Psalm 75*
SUGGESTED HYMNS:
  "*It Came Upon the Midnight Clear*" (All)
  "*O Come, O Come, Emmanuel*" (B, E, F, L, P, UM, W)

Serving Others

Hearing the Word

Isaiah 41 is part of a larger section of encouragement beginning with chapter 40. Historically, these are the prophet's attempts to restore hope in the conquered people of Israel after the devastating Babylonian exile in 586 B.C. One of the methods he uses is a court setting to contrast the reality of our God with lifeless, human-made idols, and thus remind the Israelites that our God can be counted on to come through for them.

Living the Word

One of the fun stories that got circulated as true on the Internet was a tale of an older woman in Florida who, after grocery shopping, noticed four young men in the parking lot opening the doors of her car. Still pushing her cart of purchases ahead of her, she pulled a large handgun from her purse and began running toward the men, brandishing the weapon and shouting, "Get out of my car! I've got a gun, and I know how to use it!"

The four men immediately fled for their lives. As far as the woman could tell, they had not stolen or damaged anything, so she loaded her groceries in the trunk and shut the lid. Still shaking from the incident, the woman had trouble getting her key in the ignition, and once she did, it would not start the car.

She looked up and discovered that her car was actually parked one row over. Sheepishly she transferred her groceries in her car, drove to the police station, and began to explain what had happened. As she did, the officer began laughing hysterically. It seems that there were four men in the station too; they were reporting a carjacking by a small, gray-haired lady with spectacles and a huge gun. After the officer's laughter subsided, the men got their car back, the woman got her groceries home, and no charges were filed.

Those four men fleeing from their car is much like the situation of the Israelites Isaiah was talking to. They had been run out of their homes and the promised land at "gunpoint." That may be as far as this analogy can take us, however, since there is a lot of difference between one Florida senior citizen and the mighty Babylonian army. On the other hand, both "victims" (the men and the Israelites) had in common their desire for justice. But again, there is an important difference between these victims. The four Florida men were able to go to the police and hope for, even expect, justice to be done. By contrast, the Israelites, as prisoners of war, had no recourse in the Babylonia courts. Worse, Israel had always looked to God as the dispenser of ultimate justice. They believed that God was active in and carried out justice through the events of history. To them this meant that their defeat indicated God's abandonment of them as God's people. The prophets had warned them this might happen because of their sin and lack of loyalty to their covenant with God. Now that the Babylonian exile had actually happened, it meant that they had already been declared guilty and sentenced in court. The short, brutal war and all the death and destruction were their punishment. The four men from Florida were innocent, and could reasonably expect sympathetic help. The Israelites knew they were guilty, and they were therefore fresh out of higher powers to appeal to.

God would have been entirely justified in ending the Israelites' history at the point of the exile. They had broken the contract, and so the contract was over, history, kaput. So Isaiah's prophetic words are, here in this Advent season, a foretaste of the amazing grace of God, later noted by Paul: "For when we were still helpless, Christ died for the wicked at the time that God chose...it was while we were still sinners that Christ died for us" (Romans 5:6, 8). We are not innocent victims, but sinners for whom the surprise gift of mercy is one of the true wonders of life.

Let us pray:
Lord, thank you for your mercy and grace, which is offered to us even though we do not deserve it. Thank you for your gift of Jesus Christ, and may we prepare ourselves to celebrate anew the rich meaning of his birth among us. Amen.

READ IN YOUR BIBLE: *Isaiah 49:7-13* **December 11, 2005**
SUGGESTED PSALM: *Psalm 130*
SUGGESTED HYMNS:
  "*Angels We Have Heard on High*" *(B, E, F, L, P, UM, W)*
  "*O Come, All Ye Faithful*" *(All)*

Strength from God

Hearing the Word

Advent is a time of waiting, of anticipation. The reason for the wait is because life often contains plenty of suffering, grief, and difficulties, and the wait is for something better to come. This was the case for the people of Israel after the exile, which is why today's lesson and devotional scriptures come from Isaiah 49. Yet the scripture does not describe the grief and pain as much as it assumes it; instead it talks about hope and paints a picture of a better future to come. For the Israelites, this meant that the scattered prisoners and refugees of war would be brought back together to reform their shattered community, and once again live in a covenant relationship with God (which they assumed was broken both by their military defeat and their "eviction" from God's promised land).

Living the Word

A woman told the story of her engagement. She had been hoping that her boyfriend would propose to her, but month after month passed, and potential romantic date after date went by, all without a proposal. Further, she noticed that as time went by, he quit bringing her flowers, quit taking her to expensive restaurants, and often mentioned that he was running out of money. One day when she was alone in his apartment she noticed a pile of mail on the desk, and casually began to look through it.

Unable to resist, she opened one bill that listed a number of purchases, but one in particular jumped out at her. It was a large purchase at a jewelry store. She noticed the date it would be paid off. Excitedly, and with some guilt at having doubted her boyfriend, she did her best to reseal the envelope and mix it back into the mail. Then she waited. Of course, she was waiting before, but the difference is that this time she waited with some confidence that good things were coming her way in the future. The good news is that the same day the ring was paid off, she had a date with her boyfriend, and he proposed to her.

Now, this is not intended to encourage anyone to dig through another person's mail. However, it is meant to point out that there are different kinds of waiting. One way of waiting is to be totally in the dark about the future, and to some extent, to be worried or even fearful of what it holds. But the waiting that Christians do is of a different kind. It is what we might call "informed waiting." It is similar to the waiting of the people of Israel while they were in exile, but after Isaiah told them that one day God would restore them to the promised land.

This means that they were not in the promised land yet. They feel unprotected. They are in prison and in darkness. They are scattered from each other. They are not in their homeland that has been laid waste. They are hungry and thirsty. They are left exposed to the elements where the sun and desert heat are hurting them. Someone who hates them is leading them. In a word, they are in exile. But Isaiah gives the people of Israel reason to have hope, even in the midst of the exile. His words do not change their circumstances, but they do change the character of their waiting.

In today's world, there is plenty of suffering too. Terrorists make headlines every day. People die of hunger and thirst. Wars create refugees, terrible injuries, property destruction, and death. The homeless, most of who are children, still drift on our city streets like unnoticed bits of discarded paper. AIDS is a major threat to Africa and the rest of the world. Many people wait for a cure for diseases from Alzheimer's to cancer, but we spend millions of dollars on weapons that kill instead of what it takes to find a cure to these everyday killers.

When, Lord, will the suffering stop? When, Lord, will the prisoners go free? It is a good question, but if we believe the prophet, and above all, the meaning of "God is with us," then it means that the answer is "With God, it will be someday soon."

Let us pray:
Lord, it is hard to wait with patience and confidence. Help us wait with faith; knowing that the future you offer is not only a solution to every problem, but a joy so great we cannot even begin to understand. Amen.

READ IN YOUR BIBLE: *Romans 12:9-16*   **December 18, 2005**
SUGGESTED PSALM: *Psalm 138*
SUGGESTED HYMNS:
  "O Little Town of Bethlehem" *(All)*
  "Infant Holy, Infant Lowly" *(B, F, L, P, UM, W)*

Hope for Those Who Suffer

Hearing the Word

Paul's words in Romans 12 are a collection of sayings and wise advice, similar to Proverbs. The reason that this selection of scripture is linked with today's lesson scripture is because it includes verses 12 and 13 about being hopeful and patient in difficult times. The famous "suffering servant" passage of Isaiah (from today's lesson scripture) also deals with suffering; in this case, the suffering servant (who Christians now understand as Jesus). The suffering servant's suffering comes as a result of the people's sin; the suffering servant bears the consequences of sin on behalf of the people.

Living the Word

Two frogs leaped into the distance, but by chance, they happened to land in a deep pitcher of cream. As the bottom was out of reach and the sides were slippery, they could quickly see that they had no way to hop out.

One of the frogs was an optimist, and the other a pessimist. The pessimist, sure that they were doomed, soon gave up swimming, said "Good-bye sweet life," and perished in the depths.

However, the optimist was not one to give up. Even though his circumstances looked bleak, he was determined to keep swimming as long as possible and try to think up a solution. What he didn't realize at first was that his swimming stirred the cream until gradually it became more and more solid like butter. Soon he crawled out onto the butter and hopped to freedom.

The moral of the story: If you can't hop out, keep swimming around.

In today's scripture, Paul says, "Be patient in your troubles"

(Romans 12:12). Perhaps that could be the motto for the frog that kept swimming. He was in trouble, and even though there was no obvious solution, he simply continued to "tread water." The other frog, by contrast, had no hope, no patience, and no will to continue.

"Be patient in your troubles," Paul advises. Well, to be honest, that is easier said than done. Often it is the kind of thing that people without major problems say to people who do have them. But Paul was a problem veteran. He endured prison, shipwrecks, and much more. He is no whippersnapper thinking he has the world by the tail, reeking confidence about how everyone else should live. This is a word of advice that he has earned the right, the hard way, to give.

So let's take a closer look at Paul's idea. "Be patient in your troubles." Most of the time when we have troubles, we are impatient for them to end. We want to live in good circumstances, and so it is natural to focus on the "problems" that are keeping us from that goal. The result of focusing on the negative aspects of our lives usually manufactures unhappiness and even depression; we respond emotionally and spiritually not merely to reality, but to our *perception* and *interpretation* of it.

On the other hand, to "be patient in our troubles" means that we must have some idea that we are waiting for something better. In a word, that is what it means to have hope; we hope because we can imagine something better. But patience in our troubles does not come from imagination alone. It comes from the conviction that God is going to bring about something better.

Many troubles in life do have the capacity to drain life of its joy and pleasure. Sometimes we do it by focusing too much on our troubles instead of on our blessings, but sometimes we are just overwhelmed by troubles too—anybody would be if faced with similar circumstances. But whether we manage to "be patient" in our troubles, or whether they really get us down, God is working to bring about a better reality. It does not depend on us; it depends on God, which is why we can have utter confidence and hope in God's future. That is one reason why Jesus was born; it was God's way of realizing the hopes of the world, and in Christ, whether we manage to be patient or not, all of our hopes will indeed one day be fulfilled.

Let us pray:
Lord, keep hope alive in us, and patience with the circumstances of our lives that we define as "troubles." Help us focus on the good gifts we have received, and the ultimate good you are already doing for us through Christ. Amen.

READ IN YOUR BIBLE: *Isaiah 52:7-12*　　　December 25, 2005
SUGGESTED PSALM: *Psalm 100*
SUGGESTED HYMNS:
  "Silent Night, Holy Night" (All)
  "Joy to the World" (All)

Be Joyful

Hearing the Word

On this Christmas day, Christians celebrate the first of the two pieces of great news for humanity that God has given. The first is that Christ is born; the second is that Jesus gave his life for our sins. The common link with the devotional scripture in Isaiah and the lesson scripture from Luke is the announcement of good news. In Isaiah, the messenger of good news is seen coming across the mountains; in Luke, the messenger is the angel announcing the Christmas message of good news for all people to the shepherds.

Living the Word

One day I received a panicked phone call from a woman whose husband had been stricken by a sudden illness and was on the way to the hospital in the ambulance. His survival was quite uncertain, and the family was converging on the hospital, so I quickly got in the car and started driving there too.

After we arrived, the staff escorted us to a special room where families could wait in privacy. As minutes turned to hours, we rehashed every bit of news we received from the nurses and doctors. Suddenly, over the hospital intercom, we heard a beautiful lullaby played with the mellow sounds of an oboe. As a minister, I had been in the hospital often, and knew what that meant. I explained to the bewildered family, "That means that a baby was just born here in the hospital."

They all thought that was neat, and for a little while we talked about the good news of a baby being born. Then a nurse walked in, and gave us an update. It was worrisome. There were some tears. But, we could go on back and see their family member.

About fifteen minutes after the first lullaby, another one played. We looked at each other. Twins!

We walked back to visit the patient; it was good to see him, alive, and yet it was also upsetting for everyone to see him in that condition. And then, not ten minutes after the second twin was born, the lullaby once again interrupted our situation in the emergency room.

We never found out if three women gave birth within a half hour, or whether twins or triplets were born. But I'm happy to report that the man I went to see that day is doing much better as of this writing. And no matter how the stories of all the other patients and staff who were in the hospital on that day worked out (some good, some not so good), they all had a chance to pause and reflect on the joy of three new babies being born in quick succession. In fact, I wished I could have gone upstairs to the maternity floor to see the babies, and asked the details. Still, it was refreshing to remember the joy of new birth, a baby's first cry, and the love, joy, and hope you feel when you hold your newborn baby.

Now, when Jesus was born, there was plenty of stress and suffering in the world, much like there is every day in most or all hospitals around the world. And even though there were no intercoms to play a lullaby, the star and the angels announced Jesus' birth to many; others found out as time went by. When Jesus had a chance to explain his reason for coming into the world, he mentioned the suffering and the grieving, and his desire to bring healing and comfort.

To me, Christmas still comes into a world that is much like a hospital, full of far too much sickness and pain and suffering and grief. But Christmas is like the lullaby that plays everywhere, for all to hear. You tired doctors resting in the lounge, Christ is born! You volunteers in the cafeteria, Christ is born! You suffering and sick patients, Christ is born! You worried family members pacing in the waiting room, Christ is born! You who leave the hospital brokenhearted, Christ came to bring you comfort and to give new life to all! Christ is born!

Let us pray:
Lord, let us celebrate the good news of your birth. May we hold you and your life close in our hearts, like a newborn baby that brings us love, joy, and hope. Amen.

READ IN YOUR BIBLE: *Romans 16:17-27* **January 1, 2006**
SUGGESTED PSALM: *Psalm 104*
SUGGESTED HYMNS:
  "*Go, Tell It on the Mountain*" *(all)*
  "*Lord, I Want to Be a Christian*" *(B, C, F, P, UM)*

Finding Strength to Serve

Hearing the Word

One of the obvious (and rather fun) observations about the link between today's lesson scripture and today's devotional lesson is that one is the end of a book and the other at the beginning. It is just like today—the end of one year and the beginning of another. But there is more depth to be found in the message of these scriptures than that. Paul was older than Timothy; in Romans Timothy sends his greetings through Paul; in 1 and 2 Timothy, Paul writes to Timothy. Paul counsels all of his readers to find their strength and guidance in Christ, noting that it is only through the strength of Christ that he has been able to do what he has done.

Living the Word

A common question from an admirer to an artist: "Where do you come up with your ideas?"

Most artists understand that this is a compliment, but don't know exactly where their ideas originate. The truth is that some people have a gift of artistic vision while others do not. Artists with a camera can look at an ordinary yard and see a prize-winning picture of a ladybug on the dew-covered dandelion leaf. People without that artistic vision simply look at the house and the yard as they have always seen it. No amount of explanation can give them that gift. In the same way, composers have a special gift with music, poets have a special gift with words, and so on.

On the other hand, having the gift is only part of creativity. It is a true saying that creativity is 10 percent inspiration and 90 percent perspiration. A person can have the gift to write songs, but if they never sit down at the piano and work on it, the song won't

Devotional Companion to the International Lessons

get written. Some people believe I have a writing gift, and have asked where I get my ideas. I can tell you that I sleep so soundly that I never wake up in the middle of the night in a cold sweat with an idea that has to be written. So how do I do it? Deadlines. They work wonders! If you have to come up with a sermon idea by Sunday at 10:00 A.M., you apply what a fellow writer called "RIC" ("rear in chair"), and as you get to work, the ideas (the gift) come to you. If you wait to be inspired, you might wait a long time.

Christians, like artists and writers, have been given a gift. "Where does it come from?" Well, we know it comes from God. Paul understood that our strength to serve, our forgiveness and grace, our guidance and direction—all of it comes from God through Jesus Christ. Our new life in Christ is a gift. It is up to us to put the gift to work. Sometimes months go by and we haven't done too much with our gift. Maybe we need a few deadlines, but in the church we don't often have them. So it is too easy to drift along, to have a gift that is not being put to use.

The beginning of a new year is a great time to take a fresh look at the gifts we have as Christians, and also our personal gifts and abilities. It is a good time to think about our productivity. If you have musical abilities, how are you using those abilities in the church? If you are able to listen to others sympathetically, how many people have you been able to "hear out" lately?

The same line of thought could be applied to our local churches. Every church also has been given certain unique gifts, and these gifts fit certain people out there in the world. There are megachurches that can have everything from coffee houses to contemporary worship to physical fitness programs. There are churches in the middle of nowhere, surrounded by cornfields that offer peace and a small but warm church family. There are churches with great music, or ties to a nearby university, or lots of money, or a historic building, or an inner-city neighborhood. What are the gifts of your church, and what fruits will they yield when they are put to work?

Let us pray:
Lord, thank you for this new year of life, and for all of our gifts and abilities as individual Christians and as a church. Help us find many ways to yield much fruit with these gifts in this year to come as we add our hard work to your gifts. Amen.

READ IN YOUR BIBLE: *1 Thessalonians 5:16-22* **January 8, 2006**
SUGGESTED PSALM: *Psalm 63:1-8*
SUGGESTED HYMNS:
  "*My Faith Looks Up to Thee*" (B, C, E, F, L, P, UM)
  "*Lord, Whose Love Through Humble Service*" (B, F, L, P, UM, W)

Everyone Needs Prayer

Hearing the Word

The command to pray at all times, found in today's devotional scripture, is part of the series of final exhortations in Paul's first letter to the church at Thessalonica. That church had problems; some of the Jewish leaders were upset because they had some potential converts among the non-Jewish population there—until Paul came along. He swayed those potential converts to follow Christ, but got into enough trouble for it that he had to leave town. He later received a report about the church's situation from Timothy, and Paul wrote them this letter of encouragement. The command to pray unceasingly is the common link today's devotional text shares with the lesson scripture.

Living the Word

When someone we know is going through grief or some other problem, it is hard to know what to say to him or her, isn't it? Probably one of the most common phrases that Christians say to other people, and one of the most important promises to keep, is, "I'll keep you in my thoughts and prayers." When we say this, what do we mean we will do, really? And what effect do we expect it to have?

To be honest, sometimes it is just something that sounds right, because it is awkward and difficult to think of anything else to say. So what we really mean, in Christian-speak, is "I care about you and what you are going through." That is not a bad message at all; promising to keep someone in your thoughts and prayers is like saying you are willing to share their burden with them.

But how much better if we really live up to that promise, and pray for that person. A Christian friend related an experience where he was unexpectedly called upon to give a prayer at a gathering one day. He told me, "I had no idea what to say. So I bowed my head, and then I just went blank. So I finally said, 'That's all for now, Amen.'" I told him that prayers do not have to be fancy to be genuine. But he confessed that other than an occasional table grace, he didn't know what to say in a real prayer. Probably it would be a good skill for all of us to improve.

By contrast, I once did a funeral for an active layperson. Next to his well-worn Bible, his family discovered a spiral notebook. It contained page after page of names and specific notes about their prayer concerns. Some of the names were crossed off, along with a note about how their prayer had been answered. His prayer journal went back for years, a record of faithful and deliberate prayer. When that man said, "I'll keep you in my thoughts and prayers," he meant you would be regularly prayed for and remembered in a systematic way for a long time to come. Through prayer, he stuck with you and your concern until it was resolved in some way.

Underlying his systematic prayer life was surely a belief that prayer had power well beyond symbolizing our human care for each other. So, what do you think prayer does, really? What do your prayer habits suggest you really believe about this discipline—is it something important, or something to do if you have time to squeeze it in?

One way of thinking of the power of prayer is a means to exert control over God. That may sound crass, but how else can we understand it when we seek to *make God do something that we think God would not otherwise have wanted to do?* A better way to view prayer is to be connected to a source of power and life. Prayer is a power, not unlike the necessity of plugging in an appliance to make it work. It is far more than a symbolic way to say we care, as powerful as that alone is. It is far more than a way for humans to manipulate God, since God is already perfect in motive and action. For Christians, prayer is a way to plug into the power of God. Therefore, let us promise to keep others in our thoughts and prayers, and then keep our promise.

Let us pray:
Lord, teach us to pray, that we might have the power we need to serve you, and the opportunity we need to learn and grow and speak with you. Amen.

READ IN YOUR BIBLE: *Mark 9:33-37*   **January 15, 2006**
SUGGESTED PSALM: *Psalm 6*
SUGGESTED HYMNS:
"My Hope Is Built" *(B, C, F, L, P, UM)*
"Rejoice, the Lord Is King" *(B, E, F, L, P, UM, W)*

Leading God's People

Hearing the Word

This must have been a deeply frustrating moment for Jesus. He had just finished telling his disciples for the second time that he was going to die, and then the disciples began to argue among themselves about who was the greatest (showing they completely missed Jesus' message). There is an interesting parallel; right after Jesus tells the disciples the third time he is going to die (see Mark 10:32-34), James and John are trying to "reserve" the seats of greatest importance in heaven. All of this behavior on the part of the disciples is precisely the opposite of what Jesus expects from those who lead. Leaders must be humble and seek to serve one another.

Living the Word

One of the truly difficult parts of grief is when kids fight over their parent's possessions. Often these battles leave long-lasting scars on the relationships between the surviving siblings, and may even lead to lawsuits. In most cases, the deceased parents would never have wanted their children to fight in that way. In fact, chances are good that the vision the parents held all through their family's life was exactly the opposite. If the parents could see what happened instead to the family they had given their life and energy to raising, they might feel that they had failed to teach the most important lessons of life to their children—lessons of love and forgiveness and getting along with each other.

Unfortunately, the disciples seemed to show this same complete lack of understanding. Jesus had taught about radical love for others, forgiveness, and a type of faith that went to the heart instead of just being written in the law books. Then after the transfiguration,

Devotional Companion to the International Lessons

Jesus shifted his mission from teaching and healing and preaching to going to Jerusalem to give his life for others so that their sins would be forgiven. Yet while Jesus became even more radically giving, the disciples were arguing among themselves about who would be the greatest.

The contrast in Mark is meant to jump out at you like a red flag. Not once, but all three times that Jesus spoke of his impending death, the disciples showed amazing misunderstanding. It must have made Jesus wonder, "What will this world come to after I am gone? What will become of the church left in the hands of these disciples? Will this family of faith disintegrate into a fight over who is most important, or will they learn to humble themselves and serve one another?"

The transfiguration serves as the "confirming" moment for Jesus' change of direction in his ministry. If Jesus' ministry is divided into two parts, the baptism began the first, and the transfiguration (where Jesus consulted with Moses and Elijah, who represent the law and the prophets) begins the march toward his sacrificial death in Jerusalem. It is fascinating that Jesus only picks Peter, James, and John to go up on the mountain with him. These are the three disciples who should have understood Jesus' mission in Jerusalem the best; yet they are the three who are specifically named in their failure to understand Jesus when he speaks of his death.

The first time Jesus spoke of his death was just before the transfiguration (see Mark 8:31-38). In that case, Peter spoke up to show Jesus that he was not on the same page at all. Peter was thinking about self-preservation, but Jesus was thinking about self-sacrificial love. The second time Jesus spoke of his death, the disciples are identified as a group (this is today's devotion text), but they had been arguing which one would be the greatest. Finally, James and John are the two who were trying to get the best seats in heaven after Jesus spoke of his death for the third time.

So, do the disciples of Jesus ever think about who is the greatest any more? Let's hope not. For if we've finally learned the lesson Jesus wanted to teach, we would all get along together, and humbly serve one another.

Let us pray:
Lord, forgive us for our selfish ways and our prideful ambition, for thinking of ourselves as greater than others. Teach us to get along with others, and to serve one another. Amen.

READ IN YOUR BIBLE: *1 Corinthians 3:6-11* **January 22, 2006**
SUGGESTED PSALM: *Psalm 136*
SUGGESTED HYMNS:
"We Plow the Fields and Scatter" (C, E, F, L, P)
"All Glory, Laud, and Honor" (B, E, F, L, P, UM, W)

Set an Example

Hearing the Word

Today's devotional scripture includes two different analogies, but both make the same point. Our work is important, but it is built upon God's work. Thus, it is important for us to realize that God's work is the most important, and how our work relates to it. In the seed example, even though we may plant or water the seeds, God makes the seed grow. Likewise, in the building analogy, Christ is the one and only foundation, and our efforts build upon that foundation. The lesson scripture from Paul's first letter to Timothy includes instructions to teachers who, like the farmer who plants or the builder who builds, are working cooperatively with God, building upon what God is already doing.

Living the Word

We are renovating what originally long ago was a scale barn, working to make it into an art studio for my wife, Shelly. We are keeping all the old beams on the inside, and the old scale that they used to weigh grain wagons. The inside of the roof is also beautiful; the underside of the wooden shake shingles is showing through the lath boards and rafters. We are building an entirely new (and insulated) roof on top of the old one. Since the new purpose of the renovated building will be an art studio, we have added new windows where none existed before. French doors have replaced the sliding barn door on the back of the building, and a newly built (but rustic-looking) porch will replace an old crumbling concrete ramp on the front of the building.

At times, we have felt a little guilty for not putting the building back the way it was. Purists in the preservationist world would

Devotional Companion to the International Lessons

not have wanted anything to change. But the truth is that either the building was going to continue to be an old, falling-down, scale house with no present-day usefulness, or it was going to have to take on a new purpose.

In the same way, the church changes over time—or at least it should. Many big downtown churches were at one time majestic edifices designed to appeal to the middle- and upper-class people who lived in the grand old houses on the streets not far from downtown. In many cases, the neighborhoods around these churches have changed to include more people who are poor. Has the mission of the church changed with the changing neighborhood?

Most of us worship in buildings we did not build. We participate in programs we did not dream up, and we are part of a denomination we did not found. But we are indeed building upon the work of other people. What we are doing is filling our niche, living out our own place in history.

Sometimes we are on the other side of this historical progression. We live long enough to see others build on our work. Maybe we were the choir director for thirty years and at retirement we were replaced by a younger person. Instead of selecting the time-honored classics, that person formed a contemporary praise band. How do we feel about that? We plant the seed, like Paul said, and someone else comes along and waters it. Of course we may not approve of the way our "seed" is being watered. So for us, this scriptural idea is important as well. We need to know that all of our work, our magnificent church edifices, our choirs, and yes, even our art studio barns, will be changed in the future. Others will come along with their own ideas, their own gifts and graces, and build on our work.

Ultimately, we are only a part of God's ongoing work. In the past, God has been working through all those who have come before. In the present, we pray that God will work through us. And in the future, we know that God will find others, and build on the fruits of our labors too.

Let us pray:
Lord, thank you for the faithful work of those who have come before us. As we follow our dreams and ideas, help us make changes with respect for their work, and with the hope that we lay an adequate foundation for the work of those who will come after us, that in all things, and in all times, your will is done. Amen.

READ IN YOUR BIBLE: *Matthew 23:23-28* January 29, 2006
SUGGESTED PSALM: *Psalm 101*
SUGGESTED HYMNS:
"*I Sing the Almighty Power of God*" (B,E, P, UM, W)
"*God of Grace and God of Glory*" (B, C, E, F, L, P, UM)

Practicing Justice and Mercy

Hearing the Word

If you look at the whole of Jesus' speech about the religious leaders, it is quite an outburst. He is respectful of their position (remarkably), and yet he is gravely disappointed with them. He condemns their behavior and example. It is important to note that in Matthew's Gospel, Jesus has just come through a series of contentious questions from the various sects of Jewish leaders. All this occurs in Jerusalem, as part of the final chapter in Jesus' confrontations with the Jewish authorities that lead to his crucifixion. His main gripe with them was not what they said, but the fact that they failed to let their message affect their life. They did not practice what they preached.

Living the Word

I learned a lesson about church leaders while I was still a youth. My youth group went to a pizza place with youth leaders who were all laypersons. One of them was a hired staff person for the church, and not usually one of the youth leaders. He was just along to help out on that particular occasion. But at the pizza place, he ordered a glass of wine with his pizza.

Now, given the fact that Jesus' first miracle was to change a jug of water into wine, and that Jesus and his family certainly drank wine, it might not seem like a capital offense for a church person to order one glass of wine. Yet as United Methodists who are officially against drinking alcohol, together with the fact that this gentleman did it in front of a group of youth, I recall that the event resembled a nuclear blast in the church. The lesson I remember most was not about drinking; it was that church leaders better practice what they preach. The issue for them was not drinking, but hypocrisy. Don't tell youth not to drink and then do it in front of them.

It was hypocrisy that angered Jesus too. In fact, Jesus' saying in Matthew 23:3 is the place where the phrase "practice what you preach" comes from. Now, I personally agree that it was a bad idea for that church leader, even though he was a layperson, to order wine in front of the youth group. I'll go farther, though—I think it is a bad idea for him to order it in the privacy of his own home too. We should all decide what we stand for, both lay and clergy, and live it consistently—not selectively according to the company we happen to be in at the moment. As justified as it may have been to be angry with that youth worker for ordering wine, it also seems hollow for people who drink scotch and martinis at the country club to criticize him for his glass of wine if the main defense they have of their own drinking is, "Well, we do not preach against it, so we're not being hypocritical." That attitude would not win points with Jesus, either.

In defense of clergy and lay leaders, it is important to note that the standards we preach are impossible for humans to live up to. Who would dare preach a sermon on love, particularly if you just had a fight with your wife before church over some stupid thing? Who dares to preach about Christian perfection when there are too many people around who know you are nowhere close? This is no excuse, but church leaders always fail to live up to the standard they preach. That does not, or should not, diminish the truth of the gospel message, which is perfect, unlike those who proclaim it.

Still, there have to be expectations for leaders—clergy and lay. They should be high; it is certainly possible to expect good judgment. The fact that someone proclaims the gospel should not be an excuse to persecute them when they fall short. And the fact that someone does not proclaim it should not be an excuse from striving for conduct that is just as beyond reproach as we expect from clergy.

Let us pray:
Lord, be with those who lead your church, whether lay or clergy, and help them be a powerful and faithful witness for you. Help us be understanding of our leaders when they disappoint us, and recognize that their human failings do not diminish the truth of your holy and perfect word. Amen.

READ IN YOUR BIBLE: *2 Thessalonians 2:13-17*   **February 5, 2006**
SUGGESTED PSALM: *Psalm 67*
SUGGESTED HYMNS:
  "Take My Life and Let It Be" *(B, C, E, L, P, UM, W)*
  "He Leadeth Me, O Blessed Thought" *(B, C, F, L, UM)*

A Heritage of Faith

Hearing the Word

After Paul's first letter to the church at Thessalonica, problems continued there. Some of them had to do with the incorrect teaching there that the Day of the Lord had already come. Paul replied to this in the short letter of 2 Thessalonians. In today's devotional reading he then seeks to encourage the people of the church to continue to be steady in their faith. The thirteenth verse contains a phrase that can be translated either "God chose you as the first to be saved," or "God chose you from the beginning to be saved." The latter has obvious implications about predestination; the former still carries a hint of it.

Living the Word

Youth sometimes practice a ritual when they get together to play a game of basketball or baseball or football. It is called "choosing up sides." Two players volunteer to be "captains." All the other players line up, facing the captains. The captain with first pick looks over the wanna-be players and tries to pick the most talented one. The other captain picks the next best available athlete. This continues until one lone player, the least talented of the whole bunch, stands in humiliation in front of everyone. Being insensitive of other people's feelings, most captains who are down to their last choice, say something like, "Oh, no! We get stuck with (the last player)!"

But even if you were chosen by default, you could not play on either team unless someone had first chosen you. In child's play, you are chosen before you perform. You are chosen by another, a team captain, before you go to work serving the good of that team.

Just so you know the perspective of this writer, I was often that last person picked. Athletics was not my gift. I did play basketball on a church league team, where I played the last two minutes of every game, since the rules stated that all players must be in the game for at least two minutes. The last game of the season, I was the only player on the team that had never made a basket. So the coach, who was a good Christian man, told everyone on the team, "OK, today is the day Rasche is finally going to make a basket. When he goes in, be sure to get the ball to Rasche, and Rasche, you shoot it until you sink it."

Of course, I started out on the bench, but near the end of the last game, with our team already winning by a significant score, coach put me in. "Remember, Rasche, just shoot it." So I did. Several times I got the ball, and my teammates would rebound it and pass it back to me. Soon the other team figured out what they were doing, and with less than a minute to go, one of the players on the other team even passed the ball to me. When one of my shots finally went in, people who were rooting for both teams cheered, and I must have been grinning from ear to ear.

But I could never have made that shot had the coach not kept "choosing" me, and giving me another chance, game after game, in spite of what I admit was a pretty miserable performance on the basketball court. (Don't feel too sorry for me; after I got eyeglasses a year or two later, I did get a lot better in sports.)

So I learned early on, as most youth do, that first you are chosen, and then you perform. And you are chosen by another; your opportunity to serve is often a gift, something beyond your control.

Maybe that is why the words Paul used leaped out at me. "For God chose you..." (2 Thessalonians 2:13). God is like the captain, we are the players, lined up waiting to be selected. And God would have plenty of reasons not to want to put us in the game, if you judge by mistakes and errors and poor performance in the past. But God may have modeled for my basketball coach in a church league. In spite of our lack of talent in the game of Christian perfection, God keeps putting us in the game. "Just keep shooting until you make a basket."

The "game" of being a Christian does not start on the court when the referee begins the game. It begins before that, before we perform, when God chose you, and me, to be on God's team. It is an honor, a gift, to be chosen. Therefore, let us play to win.

Let us pray:
Lord, before we chose you, you had already chosen us. Help us recognize the grace in your choice, even before we had any accomplishments to recommend us. Thank you for choosing us, and guide us as we seek to serve you. Amen.

READ IN YOUR BIBLE: *1 Peter 2:1-10* February 12, 2006
SUGGESTED PSALM: *Psalm 33*
SUGGESTED HYMNS:
  "My Hope Is Built" *(B, C, F, L, P, UM)*
  "How Firm a Foundation" *(all)*

Pursue Righteousness

Hearing the Word

Most of the letters in the New Testament are from Paul (from Romans through Philemon, and possibly Hebrews too). The other major early church leader was Peter (the disciple Jesus hand-picked, even though he is the one who denied Jesus). There are two letters from Peter, and this is the second. He is interested in encouraging his readers in a time of persecution, and he also talks about what it means to live as Christians. The images used in today's devotional lesson of the living stone builds upon the mention of the foundation in the lesson scripture. In both images, the foundation is Christ, and we are those who build upon it.

Living the Word

Near the time this was written, the cornerstone was ceremoniously set in place for the new Freedom Tower in New York City. It will become the tallest building in the world, and provide one way for citizens of that city and our nation to continue to heal from the tragic events of September 11, 2001. On that day, sin and evil struck the World Trade Center Twin Towers along with other intended targets of al Qaeda in our nation. It left a scar of death and destruction not only on New York City's skyline, but also on the people of our nation. As the coming months go by, the tower will grow and reshape the wounded skyline, and it will also be one way we can find healing from our tragic loss as a nation.

Have you ever thought about how important the cornerstone of a building is? A cornerstone is more than symbolic. It is a commitment to the entire future direction and location of the building. It has to be perfectly placed. What if the surveyors make a mistake, and let it extend a quarter of an inch over the property line on that expensive New York real estate. Where it is placed defines quite exactly where the rest of the building will begin and end.

And structurally, the cornerstone is vital. If the stone is not perfectly level and plumb, then it affects every part of the building above that rests on it. Imagine if the east edge of the cornerstone is even less than an inch lower than the west edge. When you extend that slightly sloped line all the way to the other side of that huge building, think how far that would throw the building out of level. You cannot build a perfect building on an imperfect foundation.

The church has a special kind of cornerstone; Jesus Christ is our cornerstone. That means that God has the perfect plans, the perfect vision, for what the "building" will someday be. God can already see it, and knows exactly what, when, and where the cornerstone should be. It has been placed in position perfectly, so that we can build with confidence upon it.

This image is a rich one in the church. It means that Jesus was first and the most important stone of all. Jesus was God's way to begin the church. Yet all of us have an important place in the "building," too. We are "living stones" because our life, our actions, our role in the church and its ministry are actions and not things. Thus, the church is not a nonliving monument, but a creation of God that is alive and growing.

This image also implies that the nature of the church is an interdependent community. We all need each other. None of us is the same as the whole building, but all of us are a part of it. The "layers of stones in the church symbolize the fact that each generation of Christians builds upon the work of those who came before. Yet, even those who lived long ago and have died, to God they are still living stones. The church is the sum of many individual Christians who together form a community built upon the perfect foundation of Jesus Christ. God will see that it is all completed in a way that lives up to God's perfect vision. Meanwhile, it is still under construction, and right now you are working on your part.

Let us pray:
Lord, thank you for giving all of us a part in your grand plans to make the perfect building, a building not made of stone, but of lives of love, built on Jesus Christ, so that we may be part of this community that in your kingdom will last forever. Amen.

READ IN YOUR BIBLE: *Psalm 119:9-16*   February 19, 2006
SUGGESTED PSALM: *Psalm 119:1-8*
SUGGESTED HYMNS:
  "O Master, Let Me Walk with Thee" (B, C, E, F, L, P, UM)
  "Praise to the Lord, the Almighty" (B, E, F, L, P, UM, W)

The Marks of a Helpful Mentor

Hearing the Word

Psalm 119:9-16 is the second stanza of an acrostic poem about the law. An acrostic is a poem that is formed when the first letter of each verse begins with the succeeding letter of the alphabet, proceeding from *A* to *Z* (except in this case, using the Hebrew alphabet, so it is not evident once translated into English). However, this psalm is modified so that all eight verses begin with the same letter before moving on to the next letter of the Hebrew alphabet. The subject of these verses match nicely with Paul's parting words to Timothy; they focus on obeying God's commandments, and Paul's words to Timothy also include a high respect for obedience to the Scriptures.

Living the Word

A dad bought a new CD drive for his computer and brought it home. His son volunteered to install it, opened the box, and went to work. He quickly found the proper slot in which to install the card for the component, and slid the new unit in the machine. He screwed it into place, closed up the machine, and turned it on.

Unfortunately, the new part did not work. After tinkering with it for an appropriate amount of time, the son was about to give up on it. The dad came into the room, observed the problem, and asked, "Have you looked at the directions?"

"No, but it's simple. I don't need them," replied the son.

"Maybe not, but my computer isn't working either, is it?"

The son said, "OK, I'll read them if you insist, but I know I did everything I was supposed to do."

So the son started reading the instructions out loud to his dad, one step at a time, to prove himself. "See, I did that already. And the next two instructions . . . I've done them, too."

Suddenly the son stops. The dad asked, "What about that step? Did you connect the cables?"

With a sheepish smile on his face, the son replied, "Not yet, but I was going to. I guess that's why they put the directions in the box, huh?"

Sometimes we treat life as though we can figure it out without the instructions too. The Scriptures give us instructions for life. The laws of God provide guidance for what is good for us (individually and corporately) spiritually, physically, and mentally. Are there any of them that are harmful to obey? No. And virtually all of them carry with them a high cost for not obeying them, not only to individuals but also to society.

For example, the command not to steal is more for us than just a good strategy to stay out of jail. It is also an important standard for a society to uphold. If people steal from each other, then people in society cannot trust each other, and eventually anarchy would break out if people just took whatever they wanted from each other. The commandment not to steal has an important effect on business and profitability and the economy as a whole. It is part of the instruction book because God loves us and wants the best for us, and the best is a society filled with people who honor each other's property and respect each other.

The Bible is the best-selling book of all time, and yet surveys continue to show that most Christians relatively infrequently read it. There are many reasons for that, and the purpose of this devotional is not to put a guilt trip on anyone. The Bible is sometimes difficult to read or understand; it is a book that becomes richer and richer the more you know about it; the less you know about it, the easier it is to get lost in it and have difficulty understanding it. But excuses, no matter how many there are, are no substitute for reading the directions. So this devotion is meant to encourage you to read the Bible and grow in your understanding of it. It is an effort that will pay rich dividends in your spiritual growth and in your life.

Let us pray:
Lord, thank you for the gift of the Scriptures. Help me give the study of scripture the time and energy it deserves in my life, for my own good and for your glory. Through Christ, Amen.

READ IN YOUR BIBLE: *Ephesians 4:11-16*   **February 26, 2006**
SUGGESTED PSALM: *Psalm 133*
SUGGESTED HYMNS:
  "*Lord, Speak to Me*" (B, C, F, L, P, UM)
  "*Come, We That Love the Lord*" (B, C, E, F, UM, W)

Teach Sound Doctrine by Example

Hearing the Word

Ephesians (the devotional scripture of the day) and Titus (the lesson scripture) are written by Paul. Ephesians was written to the church at Ephesus, but Titus was written to an individual. Yet both selections urge the reader to grow up to a mature Christian faith. This mature faith is characterized by steadiness, good conduct, and avoiding Christian error. Ephesians 4 also speaks about the different gifts that God has given us, and how they work together for the unity of the body of Christ.

Living the Word

Two ministers were talking to each other one day down at the post office about a weeklong revival at one church. So one minister asked the other, "Well, at your revival last week, did you have any additions to the church?"

"Naw," said the other with some disappointment, "We didn't have any additions; but," he added brightening, "we did have some blessed subtractions."

Even though the above is just a joke, the reality is that some people must think that their part of the body we call the church is to be the thorn in the flesh. Truly, it is amazing how many problems one mean-spirited person can create. Usually they are unhappy about something to begin with, and then they do not know how to address their grievances in a respectful, honorable, effective way. Instead, they act out in ways that cause destruction.

For example, many times people who have a criticism of the pastor talk to everyone except the pastor about it. Sometimes they even try to get other people to agree with them, and then drop the names of those people to prove that "a lot of other people feel the same way." Even worse, some people take it upon themselves to start a petition to get rid of the pastor; many times the pastor is not aware of this until the petitioner approaches someone who supports the pastor enough to inform the pastor. This technique for dealing with problems is, needless to say, incredibly hurtful to the pastor, whether the grievances are valid or not. Most churches instead have a confidential, honest, loving, and up-building system in place for dealing with criticisms, with hiring pastors, guiding pastors, and in some cases asking for a different pastor.

This is just one way of many that a single person can create trouble in a church far out of proportion to the influence they should have. Good church members who subvert the work of any church leader do equal damage. Any time a person or small group speaks or acts in a way that hurts the unity and effective functioning of the church, whether a small act or a major crisis, it is against what Paul had in mind.

Paul wrote, "Instead, by speaking the truth in a spirit of love, we must grow up in every way to Christ" (Ephesians 4:15). Paul wanted the church at Ephesus (and all churches) to grow in their unity and effectiveness. That should be the goal of all the members and leaders alike. In what he wrote, Paul indicated that love is the glue that makes us all one in our community of faith. If we speak about others in a way that shows we love them, then even when we have criticisms, we will address them in an atmosphere of love and truth and mutual support.

Remember, don't be a "blessed subtraction." The church is not about subtractions; it is about additions. Help build up your church, and your pastor, in love. Let your words, and your actions, be like those of the vast majority of wonderful, loving people we call Christian. Work for the best, and when you discover the weaknesses of your pastor and of your fellow church members, work to compensate for those so that the body of Christ will be strong in your community, and there will be many "blessed additions."

Let us pray:
Lord, forgive me for any of my words or actions that have eroded the unity of the church or hurt the witness of the church in the minds of others. Instead, may all I say and do be characterized by love and truth, so that I may help strengthen your church. Amen.

READ IN YOUR BIBLE: *Genesis 1:26-31*   **March 5, 2006**
SUGGESTED PSALM: *Psalm 104*
SUGGESTED HYMNS:
  "How Great Thou Art" *(B, F, L, P, UM)*
  "Holy, Holy, Holy" *(All)*

God Made Us Special

Hearing the Word

The creation of human beings is awesome and mysterious. Genesis 1 and Psalm 8 (the lesson scripture for today) share this view. In Genesis, humans were clearly created by God, called "good," and put in charge of caring for the rest of God's creation. Nearly all biblical scholars note that there are actually two creation stories that come from different Jewish traditions; both are included side by side. The first is Genesis 1:1–2:4*a*. The second (in which Adam is created before the other animals, and Eve after them) begins with the second half of 2:4 and continues through 2:25. Both, however, indicate that humans have some degree of responsibility in God's creation; we are the only beings that can think about future consequences of our actions and whose choices shape the future of God's creation.

Living the Word

Not long ago, a young Right Whale made news because it was towing a tangle of fishing nets caught around its body. Marine biologists tried, without much success, to free it. Now, every year quite a few whales get caught in fishing nets and drown (they are mammals, and must reach the surface periodically to breathe air). But this one made news because it is one of the last three hundred Right Whales left on our planet.

They were named "Right Whales" because they were thought to be the "right whale" to hunt in the 1800s when they were plentiful and so large (they reach a length of forty-five feet and can weigh fifty tons). Yet humans hunted them so relentlessly that by the early 1900s they were nearly extinct. In 1935, laws were passed to make it illegal to hunt the Right Whale, but their numbers have not rebounded. Females only have one calf every four to six years, and every year more die from collisions with ships or by drowning in fishing nets than are born. If you want to see one that isn't stuffed in a museum, don't wait too long.

The story of the Right Whale is not unique. According to the World Conservation Union's 2003 "Red List," there are 713 different species of animals that are now either extinct or extinct in the wild. There are an additional 5,483 species of animals that are classified as "critically endangered," "endangered," or "vulnerable." When you add in other species that are on the verge of being placed on this list, or are suspected to be endangered but scientists lack sufficient data to prove that they belong on the list, the total is 20,509 different kinds of animals for 2003.

Here is another example that I believe we must hold alongside Genesis 1, in which God identifies humans as the "caretakers" or "guardians" of the animals. Just one hundred years ago, there were more than one hundred thousand tigers in the world's forests. Today, three species of tigers are extinct, and adding together all the other species, there are fewer than seven thousand tigers left in the world (a 93 percent loss in one hundred years). This loss has occurred since the time our grandparents were born; how many tigers will be left for our grandchildren to see?

When God destroyed creation in the time of Noah, it was because of human sin. Noah's ark saved just a remnant of humanity, but Noah was instructed to save all kinds of the animals, and God helped him go to great lengths to do so. That was Noah's main job—save the animals, and then help repopulate the earth.

Today, though, our generation is living the opposite of the Noah's ark story. Instead of saving the animals from being wiped out, we are throwing them as fast as we can off of the lifeboat we call Earth and into the watery abyss of extinction.

Let us pray:
Lord, surely you took joy and pride in creating such wondrous diversity of life, from jellyfish to whales, from eagles to beavers, from elephants to tigers. Forgive us, as a people, for our part in the destruction of so many habitats, and so many animals in a nonsustainable way. Give us a deeper appreciation of all you have made, and be a voice in this world of greed and recklessness for the preservation of the life you created. Amen.

READ IN YOUR BIBLE: *Psalm 104:31-35*　　　　March 12, 2006
SUGGESTED PSALM: *Psalm 121*
SUGGESTED HYMNS:
　"For the Beauty of the Earth" *(All)*
　"Morning Has Broken" *(B, E, F, P, UM, W)*

God Created Wonderful Things

Hearing the Word

Different parts of Psalm 104 make up today's lesson and devotional scripture. Psalm 104 is a song of praise to God as creator. Consistent with Genesis and other places where this important biblical theme is found, the scriptures assert that all of life is utterly dependent upon God. There is deep awe found in the Christian (and Jewish) faith in the orderliness of creation, and how God has set it all up to work together. It is natural that near the end of the psalm the consideration of all that God has made, and how wonderfully it is made, leads us to praise God.

Living the Word

The July 2004 issue of *National Geographic Magazine* featured an article about our sun. Even though it has been studied and revered by nearly every civilization from primitive times until today, it has only been in the last thirty to forty years that we have been able to put sophisticated equipment in a position to come to a deeper understanding of this tremendous heavenly body. Psalm 104 refers to the sun, and it was one of the first heavenly bodies that God made according to Genesis 1. From olden times, people have known intuitively that it is like the battery that makes our world work, and there is no doubt even in our scientific age that without it, no life could exist on earth.

I used to think it was a huge ball of gas that was burning in a massive space fire, and I worried that it has been burning so long that it must eventually burn out. But for millions of years, it has burned without burning out, or even getting smaller. As a matter of fact, the article in *National Geographic* notes that the temperatures on the sun reach two million degrees. Apparently a lot of the heat is generated by a ball within a ball, each with different magnetic properties, spinning in different directions. As the inner core and radiation zone spins one way and the outer layer called the "convection zone" moves another, the magnetic fields that they generate are stretched and eventually snap, something like two magnets resist each other until one of them suddenly flips.

It is difficult even for scientists to understand the forces at work in the sun, but they can measure the bursts of energy that are occasionally thrown off of the sun into space by the snapping of these magnetic lines. Solar flares on the sun can throw x-ray radiation into space at the speed of light, and events called "coronal mass ejections" can hurtle a billion tons of plasma through space with a force equal to two hundred billion nuclear weapons. Every few years, our earth is in the path of these solar shock waves, sometimes called "sun storms." Without our atmosphere to protect us, all life on earth would be instantly wiped out, but instead, the only things normally affected by sun storms are satellites that are unprotected in orbit outside of the earth's protective atmosphere.

We're just humans, but God is the creator. What we know now is not significantly further advanced than what the psalmist knew who wrote in Psalm 104, but we would be wise to follow the psalmists example, "I will sing to the Lord all my life; as long as I live I will sing praises to my God" (Psalm 104:33).

Truly, just imagine it. The Lord was able to create an object that remains at two million degrees but never burns out, and that is regularly rocked by explosions that, even from such a distance, would devastate all life on earth instantly. But we here on earth are shielded from those blasts, yet enjoy just the right amount of light and heat so that we don't freeze or burn up.

Now, if you need more than that to be convinced that someone bigger and more powerful and more awesome than us is truly looking out for us, then what would ever convince you?

Let us pray:
Lord, thank you for our sun. As it rises each day into view over the horizon, may we be reminded once again that your care for us is more powerful than the sun, yet more gentle than its warmth upon our face. Thank you for all you have made in your great hospitality to us, mere human beings, in your world. Amen.

READ IN YOUR BIBLE: *Psalm 100*   March 19, 2006
SUGGESTED PSALM: *Psalm 103*
SUGGESTED HYMNS:
  "All Hail the Power of Jesus' Name" (All)
  "Dear Lord and Father of Mankind" (B, C, E, F, L, P)

Searched and Known by God

Hearing the Word

Psalm 100 is a famous psalm of praise. It includes the thought in the second verse that "God made us, and we belong to him," which is the first part of the two-pronged verse. This first part is a more direct reference to the fact that God made us as individuals—our bodies and our spirits (though the distinction between body and spirit is a later Greek concept, and not intended by the writer of this psalm). This is the short version of the long and beautiful wonderment that is Psalm 139, today's lesson scripture. The second part of Psalm 100:2 also calls to mind God's creation of us, but in this case the creation is the corporate community; we are a people, a flock. In a sense, this short verse brings to mind God's creation of the individual and also of the community in which we exist.

Living the Word

At an air show for remote control planes, one participant was a professional model-builder who worked for a company that made model planes. During free-flying time, he demonstrated his prize plane, a large-scale replica worth thousands of dollars. He drew frequent applause as he flew spectacular maneuvers high in the sky. Then he tried a showy upside-down pass just above the runway.

Unfortunately for him, a novice was just releasing a trainer airplane at that moment. What started out to be a high-speed crowd-pleasing stunt turned out to be a loud smack. The crowd sat in stunned silence as the pro set down his controller, walked out onto the runway, and began to pick up the pieces. Each wing of this airplane was nearly five feet long, so each time he walked off his arms were so full of broken pieces it looked like someone in a grocery store who forgot to get a cart to carry out a week's worth of groceries. When the novice went over to apologize to him, the pro simply said, "Don't worry about it, son; crashes happen to everyone. Sometimes you build them, and sometimes you put them back together. It's all part of the hobby."

Most people cannot help being in awe of the human body. As impressive as that airplane was, it is nothing at all compared to any of the organ systems upon which our lives depend. Even something as seemingly simple as skin grows with us as our bodies grow, keeps our body fluids in, excretes sweat at the right times to regulate internal body temperature, keeps out infection, and regenerates when it is cut or damaged. Old layers are constantly being discarded, and new layers are constantly being made.

Psalm 100 says that God made us. However, if you understand the human body, it is not made just once like manufacturing a car. Rather, the human body is constantly being made and remade. We do not have to think about it, but God takes care of it around the clock. Even at night while we sleep, God is at work renewing our body (and spirit too).

One person falls off a ladder and breaks a leg, another breaks up with a boyfriend and feels depressed. A little boy cuts his finger, and his mother puts a bandage on it. All of these physical and spiritual crashes call for repairs to body or spirit. But repairs and upgrades are part of the creating business for God. God made us, and God is still making us. Just take the bandage off that little boy's finger in a few days. Where there was an open, bleeding wound, now there is just a finger that is pink and good as new. What happened under that bandage? Well, the boy slept through it and didn't give it another thought, but God, who made that tiny finger in his mother's womb, fixed the finger.

It's good to know we belong to God. God pays close attention to you, from your spirit to your little finger, day in and day out. We are truly in his care, far more than we might imagine.

Let us pray:
Lord, thank you for your creative power, and your continuing re-creative care. For without you we would quickly fall apart in mind and body, but with you we are renewed, refreshed, and given what we need to live another day. Thank you, Lord. Amen.

READ IN YOUR BIBLE: *Psalm 150*   March 26, 2006
SUGGESTED PSALM: *Psalm 149*
SUGGESTED HYMNS:
  "Praise to the Lord, the Almighty" *(B, E, F, L, P, UM, W)*
  "Amazing Grace" *(All)*

Worthy of Praise

Hearing the Word

Psalms 146, 147, 148, 149, and 150 are all called "hallelujah psalms" because they begin and end with the same word we might translate "hallelujah," which is a call to "praise the Lord" (and it is thus translated that way in English). Psalm 145 is also a psalm of praise to God, but it has the added interest of being an "acrostic" (a psalm whose verses each begin with the letters of the Hebrew alphabet arranged in order). Some of the instruments mentioned in Psalm 150 have been depicted in pictures or have been found by archaeologists in tombs; suffice it to say that they literally believed in using instruments in their worship of God.

Living the Word

Mick and Molly were looking for a special way to celebrate their fiftieth anniversary. Molly, the adventuresome one, thought they should go on their first-ever plane ride. The only problem was that Mick found out how much it cost and was determined not to spend that money when a car was perfectly good to get you from one place to another. Both were stubborn, though, and so this conversation went on for weeks leading up to their big day.

When their anniversary day came, they had not agreed on any kind of solution, so their kids took them to a local carnival. As it turned out, there was a stunt pilot giving plane rides for only fifty dollars each. Molly's eyes lit up, and she turned to ask Mick. "That's only a dollar for each year we've been married," she begged.

However, he was resolute in his determination. "Fifty bucks is still fifty bucks," he exclaimed. Maybe it is perfectly obvious to you and doesn't need to be said, but this comment did not get their fiftieth anniversary off to the best start it could have had.

It so happened that the pilot overheard their conversation. "I'll tell you what," he said. "Since it's your anniversary, I'll let both of you ride for the price of one, fifty dollars. And what's more, I'll do a few special stunts and if you go through those without a whoop or any other sound, I'll let you ride for free."

And so it was agreed. The stunt pilot took them up on one loop after another, one twisting dive after another, without a sound from the back. Molly didn't speak because she was so irritated with Mick, and Mick did not speak because he was such a tightwad. So the pilot flew them straight up until the plane stalled out. Then, as it plummeted down to earth, he let it go into a horizontal spin for over a thousand feet. Finally, he pulled it out of the harrowing fall and into an upside down rolling loop. Still, not a peep. Finally he landed, and turned to speak with his passengers. To his horror, only Molly was sitting in the back. "Where's Mick?" he said.

Molly calmly replied that he had fallen out sometime during the first upside down maneuver. The pilot, incredulous, asked, "Why didn't you say something?"

"Oh," she replied, "you know; fifty bucks is fifty bucks."

One thing we can learn from this story is that too often, we are even tighter with our praise than with our money. After all, what does God have to do to get a compliment out of us? Just imagine you had never seen a star, and then you went out and saw a whole sky full. Just imagine you had been alone your whole life, and then you were given a dear friend. What if you never had laughed, but then had a chance to watch a couple of kittens play? Suppose you had never thought much about the beauty and wonder of God, but then watched the sun set over the mountains?

God is like the pilot, taking us on a breathtaking, wonderful ride we call life. We should be "ooing" and "ahhing" all the way through, saying "Thank you" and "Praise be to God" for all our blessings, for all the wonder, and most of all, for all of God's mercy and grace and love. Praise the Lord!

Let us pray:

Lord, thank you for all you have done. Forgive us for griping, complaining, and walking right by your miracles without even noticing. Help us receive and celebrate all the joy and wonder you intend to pour into our lives on a daily basis. Thank you for all you have done. Amen.

READ IN YOUR BIBLE: *Psalm 22:1-11*
SUGGESTED PSALM: *Psalm 22:22-31*
SUGGESTED HYMNS:
   "Have Thine Own Way, Lord" *(B, C, F, UM)*
   "Immortal, Invisible, God Only Wise" *(B, E, F, L, P, UM, W)*

April 2, 2006

Living with Tragedy

Hearing the Word

Psalm 22 is the traditional psalm that Jewish people used when death was near. Jesus, when he was near death on the cross, quoted the first verse of it, and by implication, thought of the rest of it, when he said, "My God, my God, why have you forsaken me?" The psalm goes on to express the feelings of abandonment in detail, but then it ends with words of confidence in God and in God's saving power. It is also noteworthy that it is positioned just before Psalm 23, "The LORD is my shepherd..." That psalm includes the line, "Even if I go through the valley of the shadow of death, I will not fear, for you are with me." In other words, we may at times feel abandoned, and that is part of faith, but eventually (hopefully) the confidence in God's presence returns.

Living the Word

A minister was walking through the cemetery next to his church when he noticed someone wailing next to a grave. As he got closer, he could see a man kneeling on the ground, crying out, "Oh George, George. Why did you have to die so young?"

So the minister asked, "Excuse me, sir, but it sounds like George's death was a real tragedy for you. Was he your son?"

"No," the man replied, "George was my wife's first husband. If only he had not died, I would be a happy man today."

The "why" question is just a part of any tragedy. How are we to deal with the natural-to-ask, difficult-to-answer question of "why?"

We need to take seriously the phrase above, "difficult to answer." To really know the answer and be able to explain the complexities of why some good people die young while some evil people seem to live on and on, we would have to know what God knows, right? Not pretend to know, or think we know, but we would have to truly know. We are like clay pots guessing about why the potter made us this way. It is therefore fine, and most appropriate, to stand silent in the face of the question.

So silence and thought and prayer are actually pretty good responses to the "why" question. Job's friends were at their best when they just sat with him, silently, in the ashes. In those moments, they were truly helping him know he was not alone. But then they opened their mouths and offered answers to the "why" question. They all had different ideas, and some of their theories were really pretty good. But none of their explanations for Job's suffering made Job feel any better. He was angry with them for not understanding him; instead, they were really just trying to explain away his troubles, and in so doing, were actually refusing to "walk through the valley of the shadow of death" with him. Then, God came down and made it clear that none of their ideas were right. God didn't come to settle the argument about the right theory of why suffering and tragedy happen, but instead God forcefully made the point that God is God, and we are not.

On the cross, Jesus exclaimed, "My God, my God, why have you forsaken (or abandoned) me?" Jesus asked the "why" question, so it is not wrong to ask it, and to feel that way. Probably the most unhelpful way to respond is to give artificial answers that actually harm because they anger or upset the victims. For example, "God must have loved George more than we did." Well, is death really a tug of war between God and us, where God is against us? Better to be silent than to be wrong and misleading.

Try to balance the "why tragedy" question with the "why blessings" question. No, we did not do anything to deserve tragedy, but we did not do anything to deserve our blessings, either. We can ask "Why am I so blessed; what have I done to deserve my blessings?" Again, we have no good answer, but it too is a good question. We would love to have the answers, but we must remember which we are, the potter, or the clay pot.

Let us pray:
Lord, even when we cannot understand the reasons for the tragedies of this life, help us still feel your love at work, and the support of our family and friends. Through Christ we pray, Amen.

READ IN YOUR BIBLE: *Job 36:24-33* **April 9, 2006**
SUGGESTED PSALM: *Psalm 22:1-11*
SUGGESTED HYMNS:
  "*Lift Every Voice and Sing*" (B, E, L, P, UM, W)
  "*Rock of Ages, Cleft for Me*" (B, C, E, F, L, UM)

When All Seems Hopeless

Hearing the Word

Most of today's lesson scripture and the devotional scripture (with the exception of chapter 14, which is Job's concluding statement) come from a portion of Job called "the speeches of Elihu." This person is a bit mysterious. He is not one of the three friends who have spent most of the book arguing with Job, but calls himself a young man who has kept silent out of respect for his older colleagues. However, it appears the older friends have finally run out of arguments, and so he can no longer keep silent. Though it is a bit hard to gather it from the devotional scripture alone, he argues that God is just, and therefore would not let a truly innocent person suffer. He wants Job to praise God, and in the devotional reading cites God's creative power, shown in the rain and thunder, as a valid reason to do so.

Living the Word

A preacher stood up in front of his congregation and began his sermon this way: "For the next period of time, my job is to preach. Your job is to listen. So let me know if you finish before I do."

Probably my best story in this regard is one day when I was preaching a funeral at the cemetery. Two older, rather heavy-set sisters of the deceased sat in folding chairs near the casket. The back legs of the folding chairs were perilously close to the edge of that green carpet they put on the ground at the graveside, especially given how soft all the rain had made the ground. Somewhere in the middle of my sermon, one of the sisters shifted her weight backward, and the back legs of the chair slipped off the carpet. As they suddenly plunged down into the mud, she went over backward, flailing her arms across her sister's chest. This jolt made her sister's chair do the same, and both sisters promptly wound up on their backs, still in their chairs, like two astronauts ready for lift off. Of course, it created a stunned silence, and effectively ended my sermon in midsentence. Suddenly they both burst out laughing, and then the crowd began to laugh uncontrollably, and so eventually people helped them up (they were fine) and we left the cemetery, still laughing. I never even had the chance to say "amen."

Palm Sunday marks the beginning of the last week of Jesus' life. It must have been frustrating for Jesus in many ways. Look at his tongue lashing of the religious leaders. Look at his lament over Jerusalem. Look at his grave disappointment in the sleeping disciples who couldn't even pray with him in his last hours in the garden. Look at his own spiritual struggle, asking God, if possible, to take this cup of suffering away from him. Picture, for a moment, what it would have meant for Jesus' message to have been accepted and his movement to have been successful. Now, picture the opposite. When Jesus died, he had to witness the opposite of the success of all he had spoken of and worked for. The adoring crowd was gone, done listening and ready to crucify him instead. By his inner circle of disciples, he was completely misunderstood, betrayed, and abandoned; the best they could muster was to fight with each other about which of them was the greatest. If he had hope that Peter would carry on, it was swept away with the cursing words "I don't know him." Then he died, uttering the words, "My God, my God, why have you forsaken me?"

Such is death. There is far more to say, but time runs out. Job is right. Death is a bitter pill, and feels like an injustice; it feels like the abandonment of God and the loss of all that matters. That's why I think the best funeral I have ever been part of, symbolically, was the one where all my words were cut short, interrupted by laughter. We must remember where the parade of Palm Sunday ends up. For us, death interrupts life, resulting in tears. But God interrupts death with resurrection. God has the final laugh.

Let us pray:
Lord, nobody was able to truly walk with you through the valley of the shadow of death. Thank you that you, who have experienced the pain and abandonment of it, walk with us in our hour of need. Help us support and be there for others who are going through loss, distress, and grief. Amen.

READ IN YOUR BIBLE: *Luke 24:1-9*
SUGGESTED PSALM: *Psalm 150*
SUGGESTED HYMNS:
   "Christ the Lord Is Risen Today" *(All)*
   "Christ Is Alive" *(B, E, L, P, UM)*

April 16, 2006

From Death to Life

Hearing the Word

On this Easter day, the readings include Mark, Luke, and . . . Job?! Yes, Job. The book of Job is about suffering, which seems like a far cry from the resurrection accounts found in the Gospels. In the Job reading (part of the lesson scripture), after all the questions have been asked and human theories of suffering have been spelled out, God gives the final answer. Later Job realizes that God is all powerful, and that all talk has been foolish compared to trust in God's final wisdom and power. Likewise, the resurrection account in Luke and the other Gospels is God's final answer to sin, suffering, and death itself.

Living the Word

A young man stood to give a speech to fellow students at his college. His speech began something like this:

> "You should never worry. Either everything will get better, or it will get worse. If it gets better, you have nothing to worry about. If it gets worse, you can always see a doctor. The doctor either can help you or cannot. If the doctor helps you, then you have nothing to worry about. If the doctor cannot help you, then you either will live or die. If you live, then you have nothing to worry about, If you die, then you will go either to heaven or to the other place. If you go to heaven, then you have nothing to worry about. And if you go to the other place, you will be so busy talking to all your friends that you won't have time to worry. See, you should never worry."

His ideas might have been a little simplistic, but at least they were upbeat. For Christians, the Easter message is both simple and upbeat, even if it is hard to comprehend: "Christ is risen." And what message could be more upbeat? Christ is risen.

So what does this mean for us? One consequence of this message is not much different from the speech the college student gave. Since Christ is risen, what *do* we have to worry about?

There are many reasons that we live under the cloud of worry—health issues, marital problems, employment problems, financial woes, and difficult children, to name a few. Worry is our way of imagining that things will get worse, and then reacting in advance to that possibility. Of course most of the time the thing we imagined never turns out. A wise man once said about worry, "A fool dies 10,000 deaths; a normal person just one." How easy it is to think of our children involved in a car wreck when they are late getting home, or to be certain we have cancer when we feel a lump. In life, things can indeed get worse. There are a few cases when our worrying about our child getting home late indeed materializes into bad news; hearing of those "bad news" cases are what fuel the fire of our worry on all the other occasions.

However, most of the time the child is just late. And most of the time the lump is nothing to worry about. Think of all the relief we could feel if we could peek ahead to the end of the story. Then we would not have to pace the floor in the living room for two hours, trying to decide whether to call the police about our tardy child. And we would be able to see the word *benign* on the medical report and breathe a sigh of relief.

The good news is that Easter is our peek at the end of the story. In the end, Jesus has defeated the power of death; we will be raised to live again, and in a world where there is no more worry or grief or pain. For now, however, we live in the middle of the story. But don't worry about how it will turn out. Even the end is in God's hands, and everything will turn out for the best.

Let us pray:
Lord, it is natural for us to worry about many things, but help us defeat the worry habit by dwelling on the good news of Easter, and your final triumph over sin and death. Comfort those who are suffering from losses here in the middle of the story, and help us anticipate with joy today the glorious ending you have in mind. In the name of our risen Lord Jesus Christ, Amen.

READ IN YOUR BIBLE: *Luke 24:36-48*   April 23, 2006
SUGGESTED PSALM: *Psalm 107:1-32*
SUGGESTED HYMNS:
  "God of Grace and God of Glory" *(B, C, E, F, L, P, UM)*
  "Jesus Christ Is Risen Today" *(E, F, L, P, W)*

Where Is Peace Found?

Hearing the Word

Luke 24:36-48 is the first time Jesus appeared to the disciples in Luke's Gospel (with the exception of the two unnamed disciples on the road to Emmaus, who were not among the eleven remaining disciples after Judas's death—see Luke 24:33). It is interesting that the disciples there are saying that the Lord had appeared to Simon, when in fact Simon Peter had so far only seen the empty tomb. Anyway, when Jesus appeared to the disciples here for the first time, they were terrified because they thought he was a ghost (compare with Jesus walking on the water in Matthew 14:26 and surrounding context). In both cases, Jesus responds to their terror by reassuring them. This is a common human reaction throughout the Scriptures upon seeing God or witnessing a miraculous event; the human is overwhelmed and afraid, and God (or Jesus, or the angel) seeks to reassure the human witness.

Living the Word

You have to feel a little sympathy for the disciples in this story. After all, thinking you really see a ghost would give most people a little shock. Remember that the disciples did not have the benefit of twenty centuries of Christian teaching about the resurrection. With the exception of the empty tomb, which apparently not all of them had even seen yet, they did not have much of anything to prepare them for what happened next.

They were all gathered together, listening to the story about Jesus appearing to the followers who had been walking on the road to Emmaus. Then it happened. The doorbell didn't ring, and they didn't even have the benefit of an angel giving them any advance warning. Scripture simply says, "suddenly the Lord himself stood among them and said to them, 'Peace be with you.'" I emphasize the word "suddenly" because it was no fade-in. They didn't see him walking that way from a distance, and they didn't have time to conclude from the story the other two were telling about the road to Emmaus that they might be next in line for an appearance of the risen Christ. It just happened. Suddenly.

It reminds me of the time my college roommate simply said, "Hi Jeff." Now, you wouldn't think that is a scary thing to say. But he had been away for a month, and wasn't expected to return for two more weeks. I had gotten used to living in our dorm room alone, in silence. Then one night, I was out until sometime past midnight, so the hallway in the dormitory was quiet, and not a soul could be seen anywhere. I slipped quietly into my room, locked the door behind me, threw the deadbolt and put the chain on the door, turned the lights out, and in my pajamas, laid down on my lower bunk. My eyes drifted shut, and I was ready to fall asleep. Suddenly, from just above me, on the upper bunk, my roommate, who had returned early, greeted me with the words "Hi Jeff." Well, I must have bounced off every wall in that room scrambling to get out of that locked door before I realized it was just my roommate.

But just like my roommate, who, after he was done laughing at me, reassured me that it was just him, Jesus set out to help the disciples. I can almost hear them screaming, and see them falling all over themselves trying to get out of the door first. Yet in spite of their fear, Jesus knew they did not have anything to be afraid of. On the contrary, he knew they had something to be delighted about, and so he set out to prove it to the doubters among them.

What makes this story a safe kind of fear for us is that we, the reader, are clued in to the fact that they do not really have to be afraid. True, they felt that way, but we readers have a better perspective. As we read the Gospels, we understand that their fears would soon turn to joy once they saw and accepted the reality of the risen Christ.

Let us pray:

Lord, thank you for being there for us, even when we least expect to see you. Help us feel less apprehensive and afraid as we learn to trust you more, and to realize that the more we know you and your plans, the more we may live in true peace. For it is in Christ's name we pray, Amen.

READ IN YOUR BIBLE: *Psalm 34:1-8* April 30, 2006
SUGGESTED PSALM: *Psalm 1*
SUGGESTED HYMNS:
  "Savior, Like a Shepherd Lead Us" (B, C, E, F, L, P, UM)
  "My Shepherd Will Supply My Need" (B, E, F, P, W)

Everything Has a Season

Hearing the Word

Psalm 34 is in the form of an acrostic As is fairly obvious, it is a psalm of thanksgiving to God. Beneath the surface the theology that is implied is similar to the writings in the wisdom tradition (such as the lesson scripture for today.) Briefly, one basic belief about God, in some Wisdom writings, was that God would find historical or material ways to reward good people, while bad people would be punished. This psalm admits later (past the parameters of today's reading) that even the good may suffer, but if they cry out for help, God will help them. On the flip side of that, those who are evil will be punished.

Living the Word

One of the jokes going around on the Internet pokes fun at engineers. It says, "Optimists see the glass as half-full, pessimists as half-empty, and engineers see that the glass is the wrong size."

Life is influenced by the point of view we take. It is no surprise that in Old Testament times, people of faith did not always have the same point of view. Some faithful people believed that God worked out justice in the world by rewarding the righteous and punishing the wicked. Other faithful people questioned that philosophy because they noticed that good people sometimes suffered, while some wicked people seemed to have it all.

Psalm 34 is an example of the first point of view. It expresses confidence in God's saving power. All you have to do is pray, and God will grant you safety. If you pray, God will always answer you. He will free you from your fears, and even the oppressed are not disappointed. The psalm seems to admit in later verses (see vv.

19-20) that those who are righteous may have troubles, but insists that the Lord will save them from their troubles.

The writers of Job and of Ecclesiastes disagree with this understanding of God and of life. The writer of Job created a case in point of a righteous man, Job, who suffered terribly. Job insisted that his suffering was not justified, which meant that if God punished only the wicked, then Job had a valid complaint against the way he was treated by God. He was right and God was wrong. This angered Job's friends, who held to the party line by seeking to defend God's justice (Job, you must have sinned and now you're not being truthful about it, etc.). The only answer the dueling philosophies receive from God is that God is God, and we are not. Thus it is not our place to understand or seek to defend God's justice. The writer of Ecclesiastes takes a view that is more dim and pessimistic. Beyond saying that God's justice is a mystery to us; he says life is definitely not fair. He sets out to prove his case, and to advocate simply enjoying what you can while you live, since no matter how long you live, you will be dead a lot longer.

Psalms like 34 seem to say that God is always fair and just to anyone who is good and who asks God for safety and protection; Ecclesiastes seems to say that God has no intention of making life fair, and that in fact it is an exercise in vanity; and Job takes a middle road, where the question is not answered, but we are mere humans and it is not up to us to understand anyway.

What are we to make of these different points of view? First, it is good to know that the Bible, and the faith we find there, is broad enough to incorporate and accept many different points of view. Second, surely God understands that we are different. We as faithful people have different circumstances, and different understandings of God. But no matter how well or poorly we understand God; it must be true that God understands us even more. We puzzle over life's big questions, but God knows the answers. Maybe that is enough for us to really know.

Let us pray:
Lord, you know we don't have all the answers. Help us to accept our limitations, and trust you, for you are the one who has no limits; you are the one who fully understands all mysteries and who fully understands each one of us. So may we live in error as little as possible, and in faith as much as possible. Amen.

READ IN YOUR BIBLE: *Proverbs 2:6-15*   May 7, 2006
SUGGESTED PSALM: *Psalm 15*
SUGGESTED HYMNS:
  "Be Thou My Vision" *(B, E, F, P, UM)*
  "O God, Our Help in Ages Past" *(All)*

A Treasure Worth Seeking

Hearing the Word

Today the lesson scripture and the devotional scripture all come from the opening chapters of Proverbs. The book of Proverbs is a collection of wise sayings. Most proverbs are one-liners, and as such they might be called "the bumper stickers of the Bible." They are made to be easily remembered and recited in order to teach youth practical ways to live a life that reflects faith and respect for God and other people. Many of them are practical bits of advice that make sense completely apart from any theological content (few proverbs mention God or say much about what God is like). The opening chapters are set up as a wise father giving advice to his son about how to live life.

Living the Word

The 1994 movie *City Slickers II: The Legend of Curly's Gold* has a symbolically revealing plot. In this adventure the trio of city boys heads out west because Mitch Robbins (Billy Crystal) discovers what appears to be an old, genuine treasure map in Curly's hat.

With apologies to those who have not seen the movie, after a long and comical search for the hidden gold, they finally discover it. They are sorely disappointed to learn that it is merely a cache of metal bars painted gold, apparently leftover from an unsuccessful reality game someone had dreamed up years ago where contestants searched for a fortune in lost treasure. Hopefully they came to realize that their search for gold was not the most important search in life, even though at the very end of the movie the possibility of finding a lot of genuine gold was revived for them.

One of the "nuggets" the viewer might glean from the movie is that our relationships with family and friends, and the adventures of our lives, are actually worth more than the precious metal we call gold. And the gold and money we strive for so earnestly in life is, in the end, really a worthless ambition.

Proverbs 2:3-4 is found shortly before today's devotional reading begins. It says, "Yes, beg for knowledge; plead for insight. Look for it as hard as you would for silver or some hidden treasure." This plea is vitally important, yet perhaps it is not emphasized today nearly enough. Many times when youth look at adults these days, they see someone whose primary energies are spent pursuing gold and treasure instead of wisdom and insight. These days, it is typical, in homes with two parents, that both spouses work two jobs to afford supersized mortgages; homes with three garages to hold all our automobiles, and lots of room to hold all our possessions. We pile up treasure like there is no tomorrow, but how often do our youth see us sit down and read the Bible? When I say "us," I'm speaking collectively of our generation.

Many of the messages that we teach youth today are in sharp contrast with what is wise and good in the book of Proverbs. Adults who get into a big brawl get the attention, whether it is on the baseball diamond, in the legislature, or in the church. But Proverbs teaches us the value of watching what we say, and how to get along with other people. For many in the media these days, the words "president," and "laughingstock" are difficult to distinguish. This flies in the face of the respect for our leaders that Proverbs advocates.

As a society, we have used dollar signs to redefine what is valuable, when the Bible is still true. The treasures in life worth striving for are things that a Bible open to Proverbs can still give us—knowledge about how to treat others with respect and decency, insight about life and our place in it, and wisdom that begins with reverence for God. These things are like a treasure, long buried in our dusty Bibles, but worth uncovering again after all these years.

Let us pray:
Lord, help us see once again the value of wisdom, and seek it like we do so many other things that we have mislabeled as treasures. Please be with today's youth, that they might learn, in spite of the roar of all around them, the basic values you want them to learn that form the building blocks of a good, respectful, decent, and faithful community. Amen.

READ IN YOUR BIBLE: *Proverbs 8:10-21*　　　　**May 14, 2006**
SUGGESTED PSALM: *Psalm 89:19-37*
SUGGESTED HYMNS:
  "Jesus, the Very Thought of Thee" *(B, E, F, L, P, UM)*
  "Amazing Grace" *(All)*

Wisdom Invitation

Hearing the Word

Today's lesson and devotional scriptures come from a fascinating section of Proverbs. In this poetic speech, the speaker is a female, personified form of wisdom (compare it to Proverbs 1:20-33, where wisdom also speaks). Elsewhere in the beginning chapters of Proverbs, the speaker is a father or elder speaking about wisdom to a young man. It may be that wisdom is portrayed as female in chapter 8 to contrast the immoral woman that might lure the young man at the end of chapter 7. In any case, one of the interesting features of her speech comes from the lesson scripture, where she (similar to Jesus) portrays herself as being present as the world was created. In spite of appearances, there is no theological assertion in the Jewish faith of another deity; wisdom as a female being should be understood here poetically, a way to make a powerful point to the reader.

Living the Word

According to an article in a newsletter, during the days of the Civil War, a personal friend of Abraham Lincoln's spent three weeks at the White House. Later the visitor reported that one night he was unable to sleep and began to wander around the hallway. When he passed President Lincoln's room, he noticed the light was on and the door was still cracked open. He heard Lincoln speaking quietly, and looking in, noticed that he was on his knees praying, his back to the door, in front of an open Bible. His prayer went something like this: "O, thou God, who heard Solomon in the night when he cried for wisdom, hear me. I cannot lead these people; I cannot guide the affairs of this nation without thy help; ... O God hear me and save this nation."

Devotional Companion to the International Lessons

It is difficult to imagine the great responsibilities that go with serving the country in a position of leadership, whether as president or in some other capacity. For any sensitive person, the weight of sending our youth into war, and watching them die a few each day, must be a devastating burden. Surely any leader would want to be certain that no other possibility existed; he or she would want to know that they had prayed for wisdom, listened carefully to every person who represented a voice of wisdom, and explored every other possible alternative to war. Lincoln faced and had to live with that terrible responsibility. Under his watch the nation experienced one of the most deadly wars in our history. With or without war, all of our leaders in every level of government need wisdom.

As Christians, we are encouraged to pray for our elected political leaders. We may not always agree with their every decision, but we should still support them by praying that they will seek and find wisdom. This means that we hope they do not go it alone. They bear too much responsibility to trust their own judgment alone. As those whose decisions can literally cost many thousands of lives, they need the help of God's wisdom and guidance; they need our prayers and our collective wisdom too. That is why we should speak up as Christians, and make our perspective heard. It is like wisdom calling from the streets here in Proverbs; asking to be heard and followed.

Even those of us who are not political leaders need wisdom in our life. We are often faced with significant decisions without clear-cut answers. Should we seek to talk to an angry employee, or let it ride? Should we go for a high-paying job in a part of the country our spouse doesn't like, or keep looking locally for something else? Should we confront our child about an empty bottle we found in the car, or ground them for a month, or pretend we never saw it?

Life is full of important decisions that are beyond us. Lincoln set a good example for us all. Open the Bible, read it, and pray for wisdom. It is no guarantee that we will always make perfect decisions, but it is a step in the right direction.

Let us pray:

Lord, be with all those who serve our nation, and all the nations of our world today. Grant them the wisdom and guidance they need to make the best decisions they can in the difficult circumstances they must often face. May we too seek, and find, your guidance and wisdom in our own struggles, that we may try to learn your will, and have the courage to follow it. Amen.

READ IN YOUR BIBLE: *Proverbs 10:27-32*   May 21, 2006
SUGGESTED PSALM: *Psalm 111*
SUGGESTED HYMNS:
   "Blest Be the Tie That Binds" *(B, C, F, L, P, UM)*
   "Let Us Break Bread Together" *(B, E, F, L, P, UM, W)*

Choosing the Path of Integrity

Hearing the Word

The proverbs found in today's devotional scripture are more typical of the rest of the book than our previous lessons have been. They are more like the bumper stickers of the Bible. Short self-contained sayings, they contrast the righteous and the wicked. This is a common way of teaching wisdom, and was sometimes used by Jesus too. It is not seriously meant to imply that everyone in the world can be categorized as either righteous or wicked. Instead, by contrasting these extremes, a point is clearly made that helps people look at their own life and/or behavior so they can move closer to the goal of righteousness.

Living the Word

According to a telling apocryphal story making the rounds, a wife suspected that her husband was having an affair. So one day she called home from work just to see if anything was going on. To her shock, a woman answered the phone.

"Who is this?" asked the wife.

"This is the maid."

"We don't have a maid."

"You do now," said the maid. "The man of the house just hired me this morning. He said it was going to be a surprise for his wife."

"Well, please have him come to the phone," said the wife.

"I'm afraid that's impossible. He's upstairs with a woman right now; I thought she was his wife."

"If you want to earn a quick $50,000, all you have to do is get the gun out of the gun cabinet, go upstairs, and shoot them both."

With that, the maid put down the phone. The wife heard

footsteps, gunshots, and more footsteps. Then the maid came back on the phone. "What do you want me to do with their bodies?"

"Throw them outside in the pool."

"I can't. There's no pool outside," said the maid.

After a long pause, the wife asked, "Umm, is this 555-3523?"

You can see why it is important for people to have integrity. Having their facts straight would not have hurt in this situation either, but it all started by a lack of integrity.

Integrity is a word that some people struggle to define. One way of understanding it is consistency between our actions and who we really are. Conversely, living a lie shows a lack of integrity.

This twisted little story began with someone living a lie. The wife had her suspicions, but the husband was trying to act like everything was acceptable. Of course, we don't know about her real husband, but in real life, there are far too many times when husband or wife are indeed cheating on their spouse. They stood in front of the whole church and all their friends and family and God and promised to be faithful to each other, in sickness or health, for richer or poorer, and to forsake all others so long as they both shall live. But as the years go by, they fail to keep that vow. They know they should, and they try to keep acting like they are living right as their integrity slowly slips away. First it is flirting and dwelling on thoughts of being with someone else. Then thoughts degenerate into action; adultery is living a lie—an easy and all-to-common example of the lack of integrity.

The wisdom sayings in today's reading paint right and wrong in bold strokes, the difference between black and white. This helps us see clearly the difference between right and wrong. But the temptations we usually wrestle with are not to suddenly change from right to wrong, from saint to monster. Instead, they are more often little compromises. "What can a little flirting hurt?" "It's just one dinner."

Integrity doesn't disappear like a thief stole it all at once. You might not notice it departing unless you are watching carefully, on guard, paying attention to the right way, and always seeking to do that, and only that. So long as you shall live.

Let us pray:

Lord, help me know your will, and follow it without compromise or excuse, that I may do what you would have me do, and live the way you would have me live. Through Christ, our perfect example. Amen.

READ IN YOUR BIBLE: *Proverbs 4:10-15*   May 28, 2006
SUGGESTED PSALM: *Psalm 119:57-64*
SUGGESTED HYMNS:
  "I Love to Tell the Story" (B, C, F, L, UM)
  "Let All the World in Every Corner Sing" (B, C, E, P, UM, W)

Living Out Wisdom

Hearing the Word

As the title to today's devotion suggests, the theme of the day is "living out wisdom." Proverbs gives many instructions about how to live life in a godly way, but today the devotional passage is the voice of the father again urging the son to live out these instructions in life. The lesson scripture is also from Proverbs; this time it is from the last chapter. It is interesting that the last thing that the book of Proverbs does is give a salute to the good wife and mother who honors the Lord and lives an upright, wise, humble, and effective life.

Living the Word

A friend found the following prayer and showed it to me. An anonymous person wrote it, and it seemed worth passing on to you.

"Dear Lord, so far I've done pretty well today. I have not lost my temper at my wife or children. I have not gossiped about any of my neighbors. I have not been greedy, mean, impatient, hostile, insulting, or given in to road rage. For all this progress, I'm thankful. But in just a few more minutes, O Lord, I plan to get out of bed, and so for the rest of the day you're really going to have to work a miracle. Amen."

It is one thing to know what it means to live out the Christian faith, but there is the sticky problem of exactly how to live it out in real life. The father figure in the scripture of the day was urging his son to put his words into practice, and by implication, he was also trying to get the reader (you and me) to do the same. The whole point of growing in wisdom is for it to make a positive difference in your life and in your relationships.

Devotional Companion to the International Lessons

The writer of Ecclesiastes put it this way: "Knowing how to charm a snake is of no use if you let the snake bite first" (Ecclesiastes 10:11). Of course, he is not talking about snakes exactly; although if you are face to face with a poisonous snake and you know how to charm it, maybe it is a good time to take this scripture literally. There are a lot of situations in life that can resemble a snakebite. They can hurt you. Take drinking too much, or behaving cruelly to other people, or gossiping about someone in power. All these perils, and many more, are covered in Proverbs. If you know how to charm these situations, but do not do it, then what good does it do to know how to act?

Consider the first one—alcohol consumption. A young athletic college man went to a party where many people were drinking. He did not drink and often encouraged others not to drink. At the party, he noticed a tray of watermelon chunks. He had a few, and as the night went on, he ate most of the watermelon. Unfortunately, he did not realize that the host had soaked the watermelon in strong, tasteless alcohol. Later that night he fell violently ill. He did not realize that he was drinking. There are situations in life where we get bit but do not see it coming, and cannot do anything about it.

But more typically, when people go to a party they know the dangers of drinking, and they have the opportunity to make a choice about how to act. They may have even been ill from drinking in the past; but the question is whether they put their hard-earned wisdom into practice. One of Bill Cosby's routines features a person who has spent the night drinking standing over a toilet trying to talk himself out of throwing up, and going through all the stages of getting sicker until he finally throws up. Then he gets up and concludes something like, "And that's what they call having a good time." His routine is a proverb in ironic form.

The moral of the story is to get as much wisdom as you can, but then put it into practice. After all, it does no good to know how to charm a snake if you let the snake bite first.

Let us pray:

Lord, help us learn and grow in wisdom and faith, and then please help us as we walk into the situations of everyday life to put our wisdom, knowledge, and faith into practice, that it may enhance our life, build up our relationships, and bring you honor and glory. Through Christ our Lord, Amen.

READ IN YOUR BIBLE: *1 Corinthians 1:2-9* **June 4, 2006**
SUGGESTED PSALM: *Psalm 85*
SUGGESTED HYMNS:
  "In Christ There Is No East or West" (All)
  "What A Friend We Have in Jesus" (B, C, F, L, P, UM)

Living in Unity

Hearing the Word

Think of an area within a city that has a terrible reputation for immorality. Now imagine a new church right in the middle of that part of the city. This is the situation of the church in Corinth; it was a place that had a variety of religions, a lot of pride in their thriving city, but also a lot of immorality. In such a place, it was inevitable that the young church would be plagued by weird, alternative, and even immoral ideas. In the letter Paul wrote to deal with their many questions and issues, his opening greeting makes clear that they are part of a larger movement, and he is generous in his description of how good and faithful they are (in an apparent attempt to stack the deck in his favor by giving them a lot to live up to).

Living the Word

There is an old eastern proverb (not in the Bible): "When the toe hurts, the whole body bends." We are all connected to each other. In the church, this means that when one local church is struggling, it is the problem of the whole connection. When one church has a success, it is a joy for all to share.

There are several local churches in this part of the country that are literally in the middle of a field. The community that historically began the church is gone, but the church has continued, so it stands in the middle of a field of corn or soybeans. People from a ten- to twenty-mile area gather at that building once a week to worship, and otherwise it stands vacant. In such a setting, it is easy to feel isolated. Many times these churches are quite independent in spirit, and may even resent being asked to send money to support ministries of the denomination. It is easy to forget that they are part of a denomination that has missionaries deployed all around the globe, and that all the churches working together support them. They forget that the denominational officers and staff who are there to support them in times of trouble or celebration are paid for by all of our churches working together.

In 1993 in this area, the Mississippi River flooded, reaching levels unseen in anyone's lifetime. It caused terrible and widespread destruction, in some cases covering entire towns with water. Suddenly "the church" arrived on the scene, but it was not merely local people. For weeks, busloads of workers came from all over the Midwest and even further away to fill sandbags to try to mitigate the disaster. Then for months afterward, work teams came in the name of Christ from many denominations to volunteer their time and money in the cleanup and rebuilding. Now some of the churches most on fire for missions and giving in other places are the churches that received from the larger church in their hour of need. They are busy distributing food to the starving, evangelizing and teaching youth at church camps, solving a divisive problem in a local church into the wee hours of the night in a church basement, administering an inner-city day care or after school program, and so on.

The people of Corinth were proud of their local community, which is true of many of us, and for good reason—we come from good places to live. In Corinth, they also had plenty of problems and real challenges to face in terms of keeping their message true and faithful in the midst of a culture that permitted a real variety of ideas, and we have this today too. Try this on for size: "To the church of God which is in (*fill in your location*), to all who are called to be God's holy people, who belong to him in union with Christ Jesus, together with all people everywhere who worship our Lord Jesus Christ, their Lord and ours: May God our Father and the Lord Jesus Christ give you grace and peace" (1 Corinthians 1:2-3).

Let us pray:

Lord, save us from a Lone Ranger mentality in the church. Remind us that we are one vital link in a chain of life and witness that extends around the world, that we are part of a great family that extends beyond community borders, beyond borders of nation or race, and even beyond the reach of time. May we be faithful members of that large community of believers we call the church. Amen.

READ IN YOUR BIBLE: *Ephesians 1:15-21*   **June 11, 2006**
SUGGESTED PSALM: *Psalm 90:1-12*
SUGGESTED HYMNS:
  "Immortal, Invisible, God Only Wise" (B, E, F, L, P, UM, W)
  "Guide Me, O Thou Great Jehovah" (B, C, E, F, P, UM)

Finding Wisdom

Hearing the Word

The lesson and devotional scripture today have in common the way to find wisdom. Traditionally in Proverbs and elsewhere, people search for wisdom and find it, much like our concept of gaining an education by reading books. However, Paul was familiar with teachers in the wisdom tradition in his faith background and those with whom he would have met in his travels. So he made a distinction between the wisdom of this world and the wisdom that comes from God. The wisdom he speaks of is given to us by the Holy Spirit as God opens our minds to receive it. It may seem like foolishness to this world, but to God, it is wiser than human wisdom.

Living the Word

Computers, as an invention, are what I call "almost good." They can save a tremendous amount of time, but then again, some days you wish you could carefully remove it from your desk and place it in the path of a steamroller. If you have one, you know what I mean, and if not, count your blessings.

One of the good things about computers, for a writer, is that you can delete a couple of lines in the middle of a paragraph, and all the sentences after that instantly readjust on all the pages that follow. Before I had a computer while I was in seminary, I remember retyping the last twenty-five pages of a forty-page paper all through one long night because I had to eliminate a paragraph on page fifteen of the final draft before handing it in the next morning. But with a computer, you just highlight that paragraph and hit delete; the computer does the work of readjusting all the lines that follow, and you get a good night's sleep.

On the flip side, some writing programs, including mine, have a feature that attempts to automatically correct spelling and grammatical errors. This is fine if you type "poeple," because it will change it for you to "people." However, if you really meant to write "purple," or you were deliberately trying to write a misspelled word for effect (as I did above), you have to repeatedly fight the computer to get it to leave it the way you want it. So I think if Paul had possessed a computer, he would have compared Christians to them. Besides our tendency to think we are a little wiser than the God who made us, there are other important similarities.

First, computers know nothing unless they are first given the information in the form of a program or other instructions. Otherwise, they are a series of switches, mechanical parts, and electrical impulses. The only way that translates to the letter "e" on a screen is because some human being put the program into it to enable it to show a letter "e" on the screen. In the same way, Paul is saying that humans cannot go get wisdom on our own. God gives it to us. We have to open our minds to receive it, and then God gives it to us. Wisdom is not what we achieve; it is what God gives.

Second, the language computers use is entirely different than the language we use. A computer communicates by a series of electrical impulses that are either on or off. Imagine a bank of eight or sixteen or even one hundred twenty-eight light switches on the wall in a row. They can be in any combination of up and down, on or off; these combinations are the computer's alphabet. A very long string of either "on" or "off" values tells every single pixel on a computer screen either to light up or remain off, and if you tell enough of them in the right combination to do that, you and I see a letter "e." By comparison, we who are reading this speak English. Computers look like they speak English too, but they have an entirely different way of reasoning and processing information than their human counterparts. If we could see a computer's code for the letter "e" displayed on the screen, it would look like nonsense to us.

Likewise, God's wisdom may look like nonsense to the world, but to Christians it is wiser than human wisdom.

Let us pray:
Lord, help us appreciate the vast differences between your wisdom and human thinking, between your ways and ours. Help us trust you, and receive what you have to give us, and live according to your ways. Amen.

READ IN YOUR BIBLE: *Matthew 13:3-9*   June 18, 2006
SUGGESTED PSALM: *Psalm 145*
SUGGESTED HYMNS:
  "We Plow the Fields and Scatter" *(C, E, F, L, P)*
  "Amazing Grace" *(All)*

Building Together

Hearing the Word

The parable of the sower has two basic interpretations, both of which come from Scripture (one advantage of parables is that our understandings of them can evolve throughout our life, and they can speak to us over and over again in fresh and new ways). The original meaning could be understood as a message of encouragement for the disciples; as they go about preaching, there will be a variety of responses, but don't be discouraged because those few seeds that land in good soil make the whole effort worthwhile. On the other hand, understood more as an allegory, each kind of soil could describe different kinds of people spiritually, and we can then compare ourselves to the bad or good soil. The link with the lesson scripture in 1 Corinthians is that Paul uses planting seeds as a way to explain how God is working with him and Apollos, yet the resulting credit really belongs to God.

Living the Word

Let's make a few observations about this famous parable. First, a seed is truly a miracle. Farmers buy kernels of corn to plant by the bagful, yet as seemingly small and simple and common as are corn kernels, there is no scientist in the world who can create even one of them from scratch. We can put a human on the moon, but we can't manufacture a grain of corn that will grow a plant. The only way that seeds are created is by harvesting them from the living parent plants.

Second, a seed is the gift of life and productivity, all wrapped up in a tiny package. In the parable of the sower, the seed represents the gospel message. It is like that; the gift of life and productivity, all wrapped up in the words "God loves you so much that he sent his Son Jesus Christ, who gave his life to transform you from God's sinful enemy into God's beloved friend."

When you think more about Jesus' parable of the sower, the seeds were placed in the hands of the sower (us). Therefore, the third observation is that the seed is God's message, but it is in our hands to spread it. If the sower just took a nap instead of sowing, none of the seeds would have been sown, and none would have had a chance to grow. So this parable tells us to get busy sowing the seeds—we are partners with God in God's business.

Fourth, the sowing of seeds will yield various results, and many of those, to us, may be discouraging. We ask someone to come to church, and they soon become a faithful member. But more often, we ask someone to come to church, and they have a thousand excuses, or they come once and don't show up again, or they come just for funerals in their family, or they openly reject the whole idea of it. Just as some seeds were snatched away by birds or fell in the midst of thorns, some of our evangelism will not be productive.

Fifth, we work with God. Therefore, some of the results *will* be productive. Enough seeds will find good soil that the effort of sowing will be worthwhile. Look at farmers to see this is true. Many farm fields have bad places; perhaps a ditch that floods when it rains, or a sandy area that won't hold enough moisture to grow good plants. Sometimes farmers even lose whole crops due to hail or wind or drought or insects. Yet they are always out there the next year, planting again. That is because usually, you carry the seeds to plant to the field in paper bushel bags thrown over your shoulder, but you carry the crop off the field in huge grain trucks. You plant one corn kernel, and you wind up with an entire ear of corn—better than a hundred to one effort of productivity.

So don't worry, God will make your planting worthwhile. Spread God's word everywhere you go—like a seed, it is nothing short of a miracle that brings forth life.

Let us pray:
Lord, today we lift up those who do not believe in you yet, and those who have become discouraged or angry at the church or otherwise have fallen away. May we be filled with your compassion for them, and your desire to share the good news of Jesus Christ with all of them, in order that as many as possible may believe, and bear fruit for you too. Amen.

READ IN YOUR BIBLE: *Matthew 23:8-12*   **June 25, 2006**
SUGGESTED PSALM: *Psalm 82*
SUGGESTED HYMNS:
 "Blessed Assurance" *(B, C, F, P, UM)*
 "Hope of the World" *(E, L, P, UM, W)*

Serving Responsibly

Hearing the Word

Today's devotional scripture comes from an angry speech of Jesus. He is angry with the Jewish leaders; this comes after Jesus has entered Jerusalem, and they have done their best to trap him with trick questions (see Matthew 22:15-46). In this section of his speech, he tells people not to use titles that elevate the perceived importance of any one person. Instead, he repeats a common theme in his teaching, which is that to be considered great in the kingdom of God: you must be the humble servant of others. In his letter to Corinth (see today's lesson scripture), Paul is apparently angry with the church at Corinth too, but he indicates that he came among them as a humble servant.

Living the Word

A story has it that a new seminary graduate entered his first small country church where the people were used to calling the minister by his or her first name. They prized a personal relationship more than professional academic achievements. But this minister had not learned this simple truth yet. He had been introduced in church on his first Sunday as "John Doe," so people naturally assumed they should call him "John." But every time they did, he corrected them. "Actually, you should call me 'Rev. Doe'," he said. "I've worked hard to earn that title." Of course, this got a cold reception, and gave them something to talk about around the coffee table down at the restaurant right away that first Monday morning.

Fortunately for that young minister, one of the coffee drinkers, a wise older man in the church, said in his defense, "Well, we need to give him another chance; he's pretty green, and might need to learn a few things." Quietly, that man decided to help the minister learn. So the next time this wise older church member saw the minister, he had a chance to introduce the minister to a person in town. He said, "Bob, I want you to meet our minister, the esteemed Reverend Doctor John Doe, but you can just call him the esteemed Reverend Doctor Doe."

With that, the young minister found himself lamely saying, "Oh, I don't have my doctoral degree—I'm just a Reverend."

So the man said, "Oh, I'm sorry. I guess I was bragging a little too much about our minister. I should have said that he is the esteemed Reverend John Doe, but you can just call him the esteemed Reverend Doe."

Again, the minister corrected the man. "Actually, my title is not 'esteemed Reverend' either." He began to see that the older gentleman was being a little playful too. He noticed a bit of a twinkle in the older man's eye, so he responded in kind, "Maybe it would be simpler to skip all the fancy titles, and just call me John. That's a pretty easy name for a guy your age to remember, isn't it?"

With that, the man laughed, shook the preacher's hand, and slapped him on the arm affectionately. Just to be sure that he'd made his point, "That's good. I had a feeling that somewhere under all those paper degrees there was a real person. Welcome to town, John."

Apparently the Jewish leaders had a mind-set like this young preacher. Jesus said that they loved other people to notice them. They loved to cover themselves in the robes and trappings of their position, but they did not live out the meaning of their teachings by having compassion or love for anybody except themselves. Religion can be a way of self-aggrandizement not only for clergy, but for anybody who uses their religion primarily to gain esteem from others or build up his or her own reputation. But the point of our faith, according to Jesus, is to humbly serve other people.

Let us pray:

Lord, forgive me for the ways I try to promote my own reputation and grow my self-image to ever larger proportions. Instead, help me forget myself, and seek to love and serve my neighbor. Remind me that even if I were to forget myself completely, and be lost only in thoughts of helping others, you would still remember me, and care for me and my needs just as I seek to care for others. Amen.

READ IN YOUR BIBLE: *1 John 4:7-16*
SUGGESTED PSALM: *Psalm 133*
SUGGESTED HYMNS:
  "*America*" *(B, E, F, L, P, UM, W)*
  "*America the Beautiful*" *(B, C, E, F, P, UM, W)*

July 2, 2006

Living in Relationships

Hearing the Word

Because many of the earliest Christians expected Jesus to return any day, it shaped their view regarding marriage. The thought that this life might end soon discourages making lifelong commitments like marriage. However, Paul, who was himself not married, knew that marriage was important for most people. Besides being a source of love and stability, it was also a defense against immorality. The devotional text is from the first letter of John; he speaks in general about love and the link between love and knowing God. The lesson scripture, which Paul wrote, speaks more directly about marriage and the relationships that should exist between husband and wife.

Living the Word

A husband and wife were celebrating their fiftieth wedding anniversary. At the end of a long day with family and friends, they were ready to go to bed early. After a few moments, the wife said quietly, "Honey, would you tell me you love me like you always used to before we went to sleep at night?"

The husband leaned over, touched her nose with his, looked her in the eyes up close, and said, "Honey, you know I love you."

She replied, "And you know I love you too, dear." Then, after a few more moments, she asked, "Honey, would you give me a goodnight kiss the way you always used to?" So he bent over, and gave her a tender kiss.

After a few more minutes, she said softly, "Honey, would you mind nibbling on my ear the way you always used to?" With that, the man turned and started out of the room. "Where are you going," she asked him. "I've got to go get my teeth first," he replied.

Our scripture today says "his love is made perfect in us." As the years go by, our love should therefore improve (even if our teeth don't). So, how do you keep love alive in a marriage over the years? And for those who are single, how do you help love grow in your relationships with family and friends? Perhaps there are many ways, but let's look at a few ideas .

First, Paul describes love in 1 Corinthians 13 as "patient and kind." Often we get less patient with the habits that our loved ones have that irritate us, but as love grows (and to help their love for us grow), it is good to work on becoming more patient. Grow in accepting the things about the other person that will probably never change, instead of lashing out at them or criticizing them.

Second, grow in kindness. It may be that when you were married (or first met your friend), you never used to open the door for the other person. But add it to your repertoire. Maybe you figured that doing the laundry, or balancing the checkbook, or mowing the grass, was the other person's job, but if you learn to do it, think how kind it is to say, "Here, let me do that for you this time."

Third, since there is not enough kindness in the world, let's add to the second idea. Look hard, all the time, at the words you speak, and the tone of voice you use. Is your speech kind, or does it have a hidden jab in it? Jabs distance people; kindness draws people closer together. We can all grow in kindness of actions and speech.

Fourth, spend time together and share new experiences together. This applies to parents who are seeking to show love to a child, and to couples who have been married for fifty years. Love exists not only in our feelings, but also in shared experiences.

Fifth, try listening, and seeking to be the person in the world who best understands everything about the one you love. Real intimacy means to thoroughly know another person and to still love and accept them as they are. This is how God has loved us, and how we should seek to love one another.

So, how is your "Christian love life"? We have a high goal to live up to, but let us continue to grow closer to the perfect love of Jesus today, and everyday.

Let us pray:
Lord, thank you for loving us first, that we may know the meaning of true and perfect love. Help us to love others as you have first loved us. Amen.

READ IN YOUR BIBLE: *Mark 9:42-48* **July 9, 2006**
SUGGESTED PSALM: *Psalm 51:1-10*
SUGGESTED HYMNS:
   "Just As I Am, Without One Plea" (B, C, E, F, L, P, UM)
   "O Gladsome Light" (E, L, P, UM, W)

To Eat or Not to Eat

Hearing the Word

Some have taken today's devotional scripture literally, cutting off a hand or foot, or plucking out an eye. But Jesus did not advocate self-mutilation. Rather, it is important to remember that when he taught, he said things in a way that would stick in our memory. And this warning against sin is pretty memorable. Some have suggested that the feet symbolize our walk with God, the eyes what we choose to take into our head and heart, and the hands our deeds. The words "children" or "little ones" could literally mean children, or they could mean others in the faith—particularly those who are still learning. In this way, these words of Jesus link nicely with the lesson scripture—Paul's warning not to eat meat offered to idols if doing so causes those who are weaker in the faith to fall into sin.

Living the Word

Perhaps you have heard the story of the motorcycle racer who was going top speed when he lost control and went skidding across the pavement on his left side. He slid so far that he lost the entire left side of his body. But don't worry about him; he's "all right" now.

It is a good thing that the way to get "all right" spiritually is not to get rid of the offending part of our bodies. Otherwise, I'm certain that most people in the world would not have a tongue. And with all the sinful things to see and hear on television, most people would also be without eyes and ears. And imagine people who have ever stolen something, or hit another person in anger, or made an obscene gesture going through life without one or both hands.

Of course Jesus intended for his hearers to never forget these words. How can we forget the saying that if our eye causes us to sin, we should pluck it out—better to enter heaven without an eye than to go to hell with both. This vivid, powerful, memorable saying was never meant to be taken literally; God is not a God of self-mutilation. But God does mean for us to take sin seriously, to "ramp up" our consciousness of sin and our determination to avoid it.

A mother wanted to teach her children about sin and forgiveness. She told them that every time they were angry with one another they were to drive a nail into a fencepost at the edge of their yard. This they did for several days. Soon the fencepost had many nails in it. Then, to continue her lesson, she said that forgiveness would be symbolized by pulling the nails back out. So, as a family, they had a time of prayer around the fencepost, and ceremoniously pulled out all the nails. "Now," she said, "let's start again with a clean slate. The sins of the past are forgiven and gone. They have been removed completely from us by God, just like the nails have been taken out of this fencepost."

"But," she continued, "take a close look at this fencepost. Do you see anything different about it?"

One of the children pointed out, "Well, we were pretty mean to each other, so now it has an awful lot of holes in it!"

"That's right," the mom said. "Even though God forgives us for the way we treat one another, our sins still do damage to us and to other people. Just like this fencepost now has a lot of holes in it, when we insult each other or hurt each other, even forgiven sins can leave damage in the relationship. The point," she said, "is to try harder not to sin and hurt each other in the first place."

We hope the children listened to their wise mom. The damage is not lopping off the offending parts of our bodies—we can't get "all right" doing that. We can be forgiven for our sins through Christ, but even so, it is never "all right" to take sin lightly. Like Jesus taught us, it is terribly damaging to our body and spirit.

Let us pray:
Lord, I admit that even though I believe in you, I still fall short and sin. Please forgive me for my sins, and help me do my best to not only find forgiveness, but to make amends to those I have hurt. Grant me not only spiritual forgiveness but also healing for my mind, body, spirit, and for my relationships with others. Amen.

READ IN YOUR BIBLE: *Hebrews 12:1-12* July 16, 2006
SUGGESTED PSALM: *Psalm 51:1-17*
SUGGESTED HYMNS:
  "Faith of Our Fathers" *(B, C, F, L, UM, W)*
  "Love Divine, All Loves Excelling" *(All)*

Called to Win

Hearing the Word

Today's devotional text from Hebrews, and the lesson text from Paul's first letter to the Corinthians are linked by the image of a runner seeking to win a race. The runner must forget every obstacle and focus on the win that he or she hopes to achieve. In the letter to the Hebrews, the intended audience was Christians who were in danger of giving up their faith because they were faced with suffering and persecution. This image of a runner would tell them to focus on their heavenly reward and overcome the obstacles to a good Christian life. The reference to the cloud of witnesses would bolster this image; it "puts important people in the grandstand" who are rooting for us and who have been an inspiration to us.

Living the Word

A preaching professor once encouraged his students to "stack the balcony." He explained that while most of the churches we would go to would not have a balcony, in our minds we should envision a diverse and interested crowd of people who would be listening to every word we say. He said there should always be people of color in our crowd, even if we serve a place where everyone in the whole county is Caucasian. In addition, there should be people who have all kinds of handicapping conditions. There should be rich people and poor people, well-churched people and unchurched people, single people and married people, young people and old people. There should be Democrats, Republicans, and even a few Independents sprinkled in for good measure. There should be Americans and Russians, political leaders and starving children, real estate tycoons and the homeless. In short, he said, don't just preach to the crowd of people who are just like you, but envision what the gospel means to others (either as a challenge or as a comfort).

He concluded by telling us to remember to put him in the balcony too, so he could look down on every single sermon and make sure that we had truly grappled with the Scripture each week and given the sermon plenty of work so that we would never bore anyone, never be half-baked in our ideas, and never compromise the good news of the gospel.

I can't say that I have pictured this professor in the "balcony" every week, but I have never forgotten his point. When we think of others who are not present as far as our eyes can see, their life and witness can certainly have an effect on our performance here on earth. We can and should be inspired by them, and strive to reach higher levels of "performance" because of having known, or known of, those persons.

It is not uncommon for athletes to say that they devoted a particularly inspired athletic performance to a deceased loved one, and that they had the feeling that the person was watching them from above. Now the writer of Hebrews does not state that this cloud of witnesses is actually "watching us." The writer simply does not comment about their experience on the other side of death. But whether or not they are rooting for us from some unseen place, we can still be inspired by the life and witness of others who have gone before us. In fact, knowing and striving to live up to the accomplishments of others is one of the great resources of our faith.

Living the Christian faith in this life is like a race. We are the runners, and we should strive to be strong, to focus on the finish line, and to do our best. We should look over at the grandstands once in a while, too. All the people from the preacher's imaginary balcony at church are right there in your grandstand too, symbolizing the great diversity and great courage of those in the community of faith. A great cloud of faithful witnesses surrounds us. May the way we run the race today make us worthy to take our place with that crowd one day.

Let us pray:
Lord, thank you for those who have come before us in every time and place, and for the richness of their Christian faith and witness. Inspire us by their example, and help us run the race in life that shows a single-mindedness of faith, and a love for you and others. Amen.

READ IN YOUR BIBLE: *1 Corinthians 12:27-31*   July 23, 2006
SUGGESTED PSALM: *Psalm 80*
SUGGESTED HYMNS:
 "Come, We That Love the Lord" *(B, C, E, F, UM, W)*
 "Blest Be the Tie That Binds" *(B, C, F, L, P, UM)*

All for One

Hearing the Word

You don't have to read between the lines very carefully at all to see that when Paul wrote his letter to the church at Corinth, he was writing to a church that was divided. Apparently one of the causes was people who spoke in tongues, and therefore felt themselves different (and superior) to those who did not speak in tongues. In addition, the other distinctions among them (slave, free, Jew, Gentile, teacher, apostle, and so on) had served to divide them. He therefore compares them all to different "parts" of one body that need each other to function. The lesson scripture picks up the same theme, except it appears a bit earlier in the same chapter. Remember that this chapter leads up to his famous "love chapter." To unite them all, different as they were, into one body, they needed love.

Living the Word

Discovery magazine once included an article about a man who studied ants. He wanted to know more about how ants lived under the ground, but he could not find a good way to study them in that environment. If you try to dig down into an ant hill, the delicate tunnels are easily crushed. So he developed a technique of pouring a liquid plaster-like compound into the top, and then once it hardened, he carefully dug it out of the ground. He discovered that the homes that ants build under the ground are hardly random tunnels. They are well organized; each species has it's own underground shape. Moreover, as a nest ages, it grows and expands in a predictable way according to the needs of the whole colony.

Individual ants are specialized creatures. The ones you see above ground have a specific task, which is to seek and find food, and defend the nest. There are other ants that guard and feed the young, and there is a queen ant in each colony that lays thousands upon thousands of eggs. Living deep in the bottom of the nest, she is unable to feed herself, so she depends on the passing down of food from one layer to the next. In turn, she lays the eggs that will eventually replace those ants that have died and also help the colony to grow and expand. Various species of ants have adapted to all sorts of places and food types. Some ants actually farm other insects such as aphids for their nutritious bodily excretions; some ants cut leaves into small pieces and carry them far across the forest floor; some ants attack bugs, scorpions, and even small animals for food. Yet no matter what species of ant you study, they all have one thing in common; in spite of their diverse capabilities, all of the ants work for the good of all the others in the colony. There is no such thing as selfishness in the ant world.

Even though they are not too welcome at church picnics, they would make a great symbol of the church. In the church, Paul pointed out that we have many different abilities. Some are preachers, some are teachers, some are treasurers, some are musicians, some are youth leaders, some are cooks, some are visionaries, and some are practical. Some love spontaneity and speaking in tongues, and some appreciate an ordered worship service and the gift of quiet prayer. But all of these gifts have their place if they are put to work serving the community.

If you like working jigsaw puzzles, then you know that losing one piece of a thousand-piece puzzle leaves the entire picture incomplete; that one piece cannot be replaced. It had its own special qualities, and it needed all the others to make a complete picture.

So it is that since the beginning of time, there has only been one you, only one person with the unique combination of relationships, gifts, abilities, opportunities, and resources that you have. There has never been another one just like you, and there never will be again. Together, all of you are the body of Christ, and each one is an irreplaceable part of it.

Let us pray:
Lord, thank you for the gifts you have invested in me. May I discover them and use them, for the good of those in my community and for your greater glory. Remind me how much I depend on the gifts of others, and help me be a person who works well, in a spirit of love and cooperation, with others. Amen.

READ IN YOUR BIBLE: *John 3:16-21* **July 30, 2006**
SUGGESTED PSALM: *Psalm 115*
SUGGESTED HYMNS:
 "More Love to Thee, O Christ" *(B, C, F, P, UM)*
 "There Is a Wideness in God's Mercy" *(All)*

Love Comes First

Hearing the Word

John 3:16-21 is part of the larger story of Jesus and Nicodemus. Nicodemus was a seeker. He was one of the Pharisees, but in coming to ask Jesus questions he did not appear to have an ulterior motive (to trap Jesus like the questioners in Matthew, Mark, and Luke usually wanted to do). Instead, Nicodemus came to see Jesus at night, presumably because he knew his group would have disapproved of him for seeking to know more of Jesus and his ways. Unfortunately, the encounter ends before we know what kind of response Nicodemus had. Did he follow Jesus, or just go home and think about it? Maybe the open-ended nature of it is meant to invite the reader to decide how to respond instead of worrying about how Nicodemus responded.

Living the Word

Passed around on the Internet was a long list of sentences, apparently typed out by a parent paying penance for complaining about his/her child. The sentence, written perhaps a hundred times, said, "I promise never to complain about my children again."

At the end of the long line of sentences was a photograph of a smiling teenager. I think it was a girl, but it was hard to tell. Her face was literally covered with piercings and metal jewelry. A bull-style ring ran through her nose, and then the edges of each nostril were lined with closely spaced small rings. Every available spot in both ears had been pierced. There must have been twenty or twenty-five straight pin piercings in each eyebrow. Literally every place that you could pinch a little skin, there was another piercing. Her hair was a bright point, though. It was bright orange in places, bright pink in others; just about every color in the rainbow was in there, as long as it shouted in a florescent, psychedelic voice.

Today, there are many people who reject the traditional church way of doing things. They have not been born and raised in a church environment, or if they have, they do not find it fulfilling. So they either stay away from church altogether, or try other religions out, or become seekers. Apparently, Nicodemus was a seeker. He had been brought up Jewish, but his faith left him with unanswered questions. So Jesus was fascinating to him, and he wanted to know more. He did not come during a traditional teaching time to talk to Jesus, but instead he came by night. Yet his questions were earnest, and Jesus took time to talk to him.

A church put a billboard up on the edge of a city, so that every car that came into town that way would see it. The sign had a close-up of the nail going through Jesus' hand on the cross, and the slogan said something like, "Jesus' body piercings were put there to save you." At first, the sign alienated me. It seemed to trivialize Jesus' suffering and sacrifice by calling them body piercings. Yet the more I thought about it, especially having seen the photo of this young girl who was probably not the president of her local church youth group, it seemed like an interesting approach. That billboard is certainly something that would have attracted her attention, and it would have given her a whole new perspective about body piercings—perhaps one that would plant a seed for her of faith and new life.

So maybe that church had a good idea after all. They remembered that there are many people who will never set foot in your traditional, or even your contemporary, church service. But they still need the gospel. Therefore you have to find alternative ways to share it with a completely different crowd.

Who all in your community gets to hear the gospel as it is proclaimed from your church? And who could drive straight through your town, or live there for fifty years, and not have heard anything from your church?

Let us pray:
Lord, remind us that the seekers of the world are searching for joy, peace, hope, and most of all, new life. Help them find new life in you, both in traditional ways and nontraditional ways, as our churches go fishing in more places than inside our own walls. Amen.

READ IN YOUR BIBLE: *Matthew 18:21-35*   **August 6, 2006**
SUGGESTED PSALM: *Psalm 103:1-14*
SUGGESTED HYMNS:
  "Rejoice, the Lord Is King" *(B, E, F, L, P, UM, W)*
  "Rejoice, Ye Pure in Heart" *(B, C, E, F, P, UM)*

Forgiving and Reconciling

Hearing the Word

This parable is unique to Matthew's Gospel, although the question Peter asked Jesus has a parallel in Luke (see Luke 17:3-4). Peter thought that he was being generous by thinking of forgiving someone seven times, but he thought that somewhere a line should be drawn. Yet Jesus was even more forgiving than that. The point of the parable that follows the saying is to compare us to the unforgiving servant—the one who had been forgiven much, but in turn would not forgive others. In the lesson scriptures from 2 Corinthians, Paul is dealing with forgiving someone in the church who has done something wrong, and he advocates forgiveness and letting the person know that they really are loved.

Living the Word

I have a rather extensive system of files on sermon illustrations. In preparation for writing this devotion today, I pulled out my file folder labeled "forgiveness." Since that is a frequent topic, it is pretty thick. As I sorted through the newspaper clippings and magazine articles and old sermon notes and other papers, I came across an old cell phone bill. Mystified as to why I had filed an old cell phone bill in my "forgiveness" file, I opened it. It was two years old, and the return envelope was still there. The pay stub had not been torn off the bill either, and then I remembered. A couple years ago I got a bill with an extra fee on it for nonpayment of a bill. Since I take pride in paying my bills on time, I called the company to ask about it. They said I had not paid my bill, and I told them that I had not received a bill. It must have been lost in the mail, I insisted, because I am very organized and careful with my bills, and it simply was not in my "bills to be paid" box.

I must have been convincing, because they decided to waive the late fees. They sent me a replacement bill, and I paid it. Then two years went by, and I just found it. I feel a little sheepish. It was not lost in the mail after all—I must have scooped it up with some old sermon notes, and filed it away.

So now I realize that I was in the wrong after all, even when I thought I wasn't. Yet I received forgiveness. Isn't that a lot like what God does for us? How often are we either sure that the other person is in the wrong instead of us, or simply unaware that we have done anything wrong? It is a good idea frequently to ask, in a general way, for God to forgive us also for the times when we sinned, but still have not realized our sin.

It may be that we are more likely to wrong someone repeatedly when we do not even realize we are doing anything wrong. Of course, we could simply be too stubborn or inconsiderate to change. Sometimes people are hooked on drugs or alcohol, and their addiction leads them to hurt another person over and over again. There are many reasons why one person can hurt another one repeatedly.

So Peter wondered how many times we should have to forgive someone who repeatedly wrongs us. It is a good question. If we really do forgive others over and over again, then will they ever learn from their mistakes? Will we have any way to defend ourselves against the pain they might inflict? In the case of drug addicts, for example, too much forgiveness can be enabling for them. If they are too often and too easily forgiven, they never have to endure the consequence of their actions, or face up to how hurtful they have acted.

Peter thought that seven times was a generous number of times to forgive another person, but Jesus does not place any real limit on forgiveness. So Jesus replied to Peter, "Seventy times seven." I suppose he hoped that by the time Peter had forgiven another person four hundred ninety times, forgiveness would either get to be a habit, or Peter would have lost track of the exact number of infractions and just keep forgiving that person.

Isn't that like God? Long after all of us, in our good sense, know to give up on another person, God just keeps forgiving. And forgiving, and forgiving.

Let us pray:
Lord, forgive us our sins, as we forgive those who sin against us. Through Christ, Amen.

READ IN YOUR BIBLE: *Luke 20:45–21:4*
SUGGESTED PSALM: *Psalm 50:1-15*
SUGGESTED HYMNS:
 "*Stand Up, Stand Up for Jesus*" (B, C, E, F, L, UM)
 "*Lift High the Cross*" (B, L, P, UM, W)

August 13, 2006

Giving Generously

Hearing the Word

The two parts of the devotional lesson paint quite a contrast. First, Jesus is criticizing the teachers of the law for being more concerned about their position than being genuine leaders of caring and love; he also specifically mentioned that they take advantage of widows and rob them of their homes. By contrast, he points out a poor widow because she is generous. She goes nameless, and apparently does not even realize she is being pointed out as an example. Her giving is self-sacrificial, even though it is a small amount of money. Pointing her out as a favorable example and criticizing the Jewish leaders is one of his last teachings before Luke's narrative moves into Jesus' last days.

Living the Word

From *Illustration Digest* comes a story of a Christian businessman who was traveling in Korea. He noticed a young man pulling a plow while an older man, presumably his father, was guiding it through the field. "My goodness," the man commented to his translator. Those people must be terribly poor. Look at that. They don't even have an ox like most of the other farmers here do."

The translator replied, "Yes, they are indeed poor, but they used to have an ox. When the Christian church burned down, they sold their ox so they could have money to give to help rebuild their church. So this year they are pulling the plow themselves."

The businessman said, "Oh, that's a terrible sacrifice."

The translator replied, "Well, they did not feel it was a sacrifice. They were happy they had an ox they could sell."

One of the barriers to our financial stewardship, at least in this

Devotional Companion to the International Lessons

country, is that we see giving as a major sacrifice. We are so attached to money that to give any of it up is painful to us. One of the purposes of giving, though, is to teach us to be less attached to it. It teaches us that the real pleasure of money is not as a possession to cling to, but in giving it as a tool for good.

Our church includes in the bulletin each Sunday the amount of money that we gave the week before in the offering. In one of my churches, we have gotten used to seeing numbers of $1,000 to $3,000 per week. That may seem like a lot of money, but to put it in perspective, I wondered what would happen if we started to put two numbers in the bulletin. One would be the number of dollars we gave that week, and the other would be the number of dollars we kept for ourselves. For example, for those families with two working parents who each earn $30,000 a year, and who gave an average 2 to 3 percent of their income, their numbers might be something like this: at just over 2 percent, they are giving about $25 and keeping about $1,154 a week. For 100 such families, the church would have given $2,500 and kept $110,000 that week.

By contrast, once a month we have a "noisy offering." The children who come up for the children's moments get to help the ushers with the offering on that day. They get coffee cans with slots in the lids, and they run around the congregation getting change from the people for missions. They rattle their cans, laugh, put all of their own money in; you can hardly hear the organist play the music, but they make giving the offering fun. And all of it goes for things like feeding children who would otherwise starve to death in other parts of the world.

When we give an offering, what we need more of is the joy and generosity of children. They give their last dime and have fun doing it. Then we teach them our idea of the value of money, and they forget the right values. So once they become grownups they hold on to most of it, and miss out on much of the joy of giving. We need to just be a little more like the widow Jesus looked at, the one who was poor, but gave practically all she had to live on.

I guess when she was a child, nobody ever taught her what we adults know about how important it is to hang on to your money.

Let us pray:
Lord, forgive our selfish ways. Help us increase our sharing until it is fun, until it is a joy. And then help us give because it is a joy. Amen.

READ IN YOUR BIBLE: *Psalm 37:16-24*
SUGGESTED PSALM: *Psalm 37:25-40*
SUGGESTED HYMNS:
  "Morning Has Broken" *(B, E, F, P, UM, W)*
  "O Worship the King" *(B, C, E, F, L, P, UM)*

August 20, 2006

Reasons for Giving

Hearing the Word

This psalm reflects the ancient theology that the good will be materially rewarded and the evil will be punished by losing their material possessions. This includes the right to live in the land. Remember that the promised land was one of two main promises that God originally made to Abram (later Abraham). Faithfulness to the covenant was thus thought to lead to the right to live in the land and be blessed; but not to be faithful to God's covenant would result in voiding the contract. Again, some in the Jewish faith questioned this link between material rewards and faithfulness because they noticed that some good people failed to prosper materially, while some evil people got rich.

Living the Word

This devotional is titled "Reasons for Giving." The titles for each devotional lesson in this book are the same as the title for the adult lesson of the day. The titles and scriptures are all chosen by the International Lesson Series (ILS) committee, so when we writers in the various participating denominations write, we begin with the committee's choice of scripture and title; then we go from there.

Having someone else come up with a title before the article is written is an interesting exercise. As a writer, it often guides my thoughts as I consider the meaning of a scripture, and it is rewarding because many times it may cause me to think about a scripture from a new perspective.

With this background in mind, you will now know that I had the lesson title "Reasons for Giving" in mind as I read Psalm 37. (The title was really selected to go with the lesson scripture, which

Devotional Companion to the International Lessons

comes from 2 Corinthians 9, where Paul gives the church reasons for giving.) So instead of finding reasons for giving in Psalm 37, there is more of an observation that God will bless those who are faithful and generous. In other words, God will bless the faithful, and take blessings away from the wicked. If you are looking for a reason to give, then this one seems selfish. It sounds like what we are saying is to give so that God will bless you.

I received a prayer rug in the mail not long ago, an unsolicited gift from some religious group. The letter had stories in it about how the prayer rug had healed people of their diseases just by holding it against the body, and so on. Anyway, those who received the letter had to pass the prayer rug on to someone else, and **send in a tidy little sum**, and then they would get a blessing from God in return. Does that seem to you like a good reason to give?

There are a lot of reasons that people give, I suppose. Some give to have their name on a plaque because they think all the other rich people in the church or community will also be doing the same to sponsor some major building project. Giving in that case protects or enhances a person's prestige; it keeps one from looking cheap.

Some people give out of guilt, and others give out of a sense of duty. But the best reason to give is out of love. When someone gives, and expects nothing in return, that is a pure, unselfish, loving reason to give.

In Psalm 37, God is giving to the people of Israel. They are blessed by God's gifts. It is easy to link their behavior to the gift, and conclude that they earned what they got. But that is actually backward. God's reason to give was not to get a certain kind of behavior from them. He gave to them out of love. Then he hoped they would respond with a faithful life.

God is the first giver. God's gifts are given out of love. Our gifts are best when we don't attach strings or expectations to them, when we don't compromise them with questionable motives. But we would not be able to give anything at all unless God had first given us all we have. We have received in love; may we give in love.

Let us pray:
Lord, you and I know my motives for giving. May I see my gifts as a way to thank you for what you have first given me, and give them with joy. Amen.

READ IN YOUR BIBLE: *James 4:1-10*   **August 27, 2006**
SUGGESTED PSALM: *Psalm 75*
SUGGESTED HYMNS:
  "*Beneath the Cross of Jesus*" (B, C, E, L, P, UM)
  "*Lord, I Want to Be a Christian*" (B, C, F, P, UM, W)

Leaning on Grace

Hearing the Word

The letter written by James is written in the wisdom style; its arguments appeal to common sense. In the case of our devotional scripture (James 4:1-10), he also cites scriptures to bolster his case. The first scripture he mentioned is a mystery; either it is a lost scripture, or one that did not make it into our modern-day canon, or his quotation is difficult to match up with a scripture known to us. The next one (in 4:6) comes from Proverbs 3:34; Proverbs is also Wisdom material, and so it makes sense that the writer of James would be drawn to quoting from it. James's subject in this portion is materialism, and then God's grace (which is given to the humble as opposed to the proud).

Living the Word

A woman and her husband were planning to attend a championship basketball game one year, but as they drove by, she noticed people walking around on the sidewalks with signs that indicated what they would pay for a ticket to get inside. Some people were offering $500 up to $1,000 for a seat. When the woman saw this, she thought of all the things she wanted to buy for the house that $2,000 would buy. She turned to her husband, but before she could ask whether he would consider selling their tickets, he firmly said, "No. No way. This is a once in a lifetime game."

So she said, "Well, what if we see someone who would pay $2,000 per ticket?"

"No, I still wouldn't do it."

She persisted. "OK, but what if we see someone who would pay $5,000 per ticket?"

At that, he paused, and she thought she had finally found his price. "Well," he said, "even for that price I wouldn't sell mine, but I think I'd sell yours."

We get so attached to possessions, and yet they are all temporary. All you have to do is attend a yard sale, or follow the garbage truck around town a while, or go to a secondhand store, or look in the classifieds, and you can see what eventually happens to possessions. Take a hard look at any possession you own, from your toothbrush to your computer. Try to imagine the future of it, and how it will end up. Maybe it will go to the auctioneer, or to a relative and then to the auctioneer. Or maybe it will eventually get broken and thrown away. Or maybe it will be given to Salvation Army and sold in their shop to someone else. Any material thing has a life expectancy; it cannot last forever. Yet we invest love in those transitory things; love, which is an eternal gift. Materialism is misplaced love. We should invest it in God, and in our relationships with others. But instead, as James says, we love things.

There is a story about a rich man who wanted to take his possessions with him to heaven. Saint Peter told him he would have to make an exception. Anything the man could get into a suitcase would be allowed. So the man sold all that he had, bought solid gold bars, and packed them in the suitcase. When he eventually went to heaven he took the suitcase with him. Saint Peter asked to see what he had brought with him. The man proudly opened the suitcase to show off his vast wealth. Saint Peter took one look, laughed, and said, "You mean, all you brought was paving bricks?"

All the material things we attach such value to will one day have no more value than paving bricks. Maybe that is why we have to leave all those things behind. They are needed here in the secondhand stores, and to keep auctioneers in business. Meanwhile, the good news is that you do get to take a suitcase with you. But in it you can put all your loves, all your relationships, all your hopes, and all your faith. These things have everlasting value.

So, invest wisely.

Let us pray:
Lord, help us trust you to take care of our material needs, so that we may concentrate on those things that will last forever. Forgive us for misplacing our love and loyalty, and free us from the love of things that we may invest ourselves in you, and in those we love. Through Christ our Lord, Amen.